'The
Economist

Pocket Style Book

The Economist

Pocket Style Book

The Economist Publications Ltd
PO Box 1DW
40 Duke Street
London W1A 1DW

© The Economist Publications Ltd, 1986

Reprinted and revised 1986
Reprinted 1987

British Library Cataloguing in Publication Data

The Economist pocket style book.
  1. English language – Style
  808   PE1421

ISBN 0-85058-087-0

Extracts from BS261: Part 2: 1976 are reproduced by permission of the
British Standards Institution, Linford Wood, Milton Keynes, MK14 6LE.

Jacket and illustrations by Rufus Segar

Photoset by Paston Press, Norwich
Printed in Great Britain by Hollen Street Press Ltd., Slough

Contents

Preface

On only two scores can *The Economist* hope to outdo its rivals consistently. One is the quality of its analysis; the other is the quality of its writing. Over the years, various internal style books have codified the newspaper's practices. The latest version is offered to a wider audience.

The aim of this style book is to give some general advice on writing, to point out some common errors, and to set some arbitrary rules. The arbitrary choices are those of the paper's editors over many years, codified and refreshed by John Grimond, editor of *The Economist*'s American Survey.

To make the style book of wider general interest, additional material has been added, drawing on the series of reference books published under *The Economist*'s imprint.

All the prescriptive judgments in this style book, however, are directly derived from those used each week in writing and editing *The Economist*.

Throughout the text, bold type is used to indicate examples. Words in SMALL CAPITALS indicate a separate but relevant entry (except in the paragraphs headed ABBREVIATIONS, where the use of small capitals is discussed).

A note on style

The first requirement of *The Economist* is that it should be readily understandable. Clarity of writing usually follows clarity of thought. So think what you want to say, then say it as simply as possible. Keep in mind George Orwell's six elementary rules ("Politics and the English Language", 1946):

1) Never use a METAPHOR, simile or other figure of speech which you are used to seeing in print.

2) Never use a long word where a SHORT WORD will do.

3) If it is possible to cut out a word, always cut it out.

4) Never use the passive where you can use the ACTIVE.

5) Never use a FOREIGN PHRASE, a scientific word or a JARGON word if you can think of an everyday English equivalent.

6) Break any of these rules sooner than say anything outright barbarous.

The reader is primarily interested in what you have to say. By the way in which you say it you may encourage him either to read on or to stop reading. If you want him to read on:

1) Do not be stuffy or pompous. Use the language of everyday speech, not that of spokesmen, lawyers or bureaucrats (so prefer **let** to **permit, people** to **persons, buy** to **purchase, colleague** to **peer, way out** to **exit, present** to **gift, rich** to **wealthy**). You can avoid offending women without using **chairperson, humankind** and **Ms.** Prefer **chairman** (for a man) or **in the chair, mankind,** so long as the context is not offensive, and the precision of **Mrs** and **Miss** wherever you can.

2) Do not be hectoring or arrogant. Those who disagree with you are not necessarily **stupid** or **insane**. You can make your views clear without telling the government what it **must** do. Nobody needs to be described as **silly**: let your analysis prove that he, or she, is.

3) Do not be too pleased with yourself. Don't boast of your own cleverness by telling the reader that you correctly predicted something or that you have a scoop. You are more likely to bore or irritate him than to impress him. So keep references to *The Economist* to a minimum, particularly those of the we-told-you-so variety. And avoid references to "this correspondent" or "your correspondent", which are always self-conscious and often self-congratulatory.

4) Do not be too chatty. The sentence **"So far, so good"** neither informs nor amuses. It irritates. So do **Surprise, surprise, Ho, ho**, etc.

5) Do not be too free with SLANG (eg, **He really hit the big time in 1966**).

6) Do not be sloppy in the construction of your sentences and paragraphs. Do not use a participle unless you make it clear what it applies to. Thus, avoid **Having died, they had to bury him**, or **Proceeding along this line of thought, the cause of the train crash becomes clear**.
  To never split an infinitive is quite easy. Don't overdo the use of **don't, isn't, can't**, etc.
  Use the subjunctive properly. If you are posing a hypothesis contrary to fact, you must use the subjunctive. Thus, **If Hitler were alive today, he could tell us whether he kept a diary**. If the hypothesis may or may not be true, you do not use the subjunctive. Thus, **If this diary is not Hitler's, we shall be glad we did not publish it**. If you have **would** in the main clause, you must use the subjunctive in the **if** clause. **If you were to disregard this rule, you would make a fool of yourself**.

Do your best to be lucid. Simple sentences help. Keep complicated constructions and gimmicks to a minimum, if necessary by remembering the *New Yorker*'s comment on *Time* magazine: "Backward ran sentences until reeled the mind." Mark Twain described how a good writer treats sentences: "At times he may indulge himself with a long one, but he will make sure there are no folds in it, no vaguenesses, no parenthetical interruptions of its view as a whole; when he has done with it, it won't be a sea-serpent with half of its arches under the water; it will be a torch-light procession."
  Long paragraphs, like long sentences, can confuse the reader. "The paragraph", according to Fowler, "is essentially a unit of thought, not of

length; it must be homogeneous in subject matter and sequential in treatment." One-sentence paragraphs should be used only occasionally.

Clear thinking is, in fact, the key to clear writing. "A scrupulous writer," observed Orwell, "in every sentence that he writes, will ask himself at least four questions, thus: What am I trying to say? What words will express it? What image or idiom will make it clearer? Is this image fresh enough to have an effect? And he will probably ask himself two more: Could I put it more shortly? Have I said anything that is avoidably ugly?"

Scrupulous writers will also notice that their copy is edited only lightly and is likely to be used. It may even be read.

A

Abbreviations. Unless an abbreviation or acronym is so familiar that it is used more often than the full form (eg, BBC, CIA, EEC, FBI, GATT, NATO, OECD), write the words in full on first appearance: thus, **Trades Union Congress** (not TUC) on first mention. After that, try not to repeat the abbreviation too often; eg, write **the agency** rather than the IAEA, **the community** rather than the EEC, to avoid spattering the page with capital letters. There is no need to give the initials of an organisation if it is not referred to again. (Full names and abbreviations for international bodies are listed under ORGANISATIONS.)

If an abbreviation can be pronounced (eg, EFTA, NATO, UNESCO), it does not generally require the definite article. (GATT, however, is sometimes called **the** GATT, unlike NIESR, which is never called the Neeser by anyone who works for it.) Other organisations – except companies – should usually be preceded by the (**the** BBC, **the** DHSS, **the** KGB, **the** UNHCR). Use MP only after first spelling out **member of Parliament** in full (in many places an MP is a military policeman).

Do not use Prof, Sen, Col, etc. **Lieut-Colonel** and **Lieut-Commander** are permissible; so is Rev, but it must be preceded by **the** and followed by a Christian name or initial: the **Rev Jesse Jackson** (thereafter **Mr Jackson**).

Always spell out **page, pages, hectares, miles.**

In bodymatter, all abbreviations, whether they can be pronounced as words or not (GNP, GDP, FOB, CIF), should be set in small capitals, with no points – unless they are currencies like **DM** or **FFr**, or degrees of temperature like **°F** and **°C**. Brackets, apostrophes and all other typographical furniture accompanying small capitals are generally set in ordinary roman, with a lower-case s (also roman) for plurals and genitives. Thus, IOUS, MPS' salaries, (SDRS), etc. But ampersands are set as small capitals, as are numerals and any hyphens attaching them to a small capital. Thus R&D, A23, M1, F-16, etc.

In typewritten notes, or when small capitals are not available, follow *The Economist*'s former rules:

1) If an abbreviation or acronym is generally pronounced as a word (eg, **Nato, Gatt, Sogat**), use upper case for the initial only.

2) For all other abbreviated names (eg, **BBC, EMS, IBM, NGA**) use caps.

3) For abbreviated phrases (**gdp, mph, eps**) use all lower case.

Although much of the Contents page of *The Economist* consists of headings, these should be treated as bodymatter, so any abbreviations are set in small capitals. In genuine headings on that page – eg, on digests – abbreviations take big capitals.

Use lower case for **kg, km, lb** (never lbs), **mph** and other MEASURES, and for **ie, eg**, which should both be followed by commas.

Most upper-case abbreviations take upper-case initial letters when written in full (eg, the LSO is the **London Symphony Orchestra**), but there are exceptions: CAP but **common agricultural policy**, VLSI but **very large-scale integration**, PSBR but **public-sector borrowing requirement.**

Write **Euro-MPs**, not MEPs.

Here is a list of some common business abbreviations.

ACA	Associate of the Institute of Chartered Accountants in England and Wales
ACT	advance corporation tax (UK)
AG	Aktiengesellschaft (German or Swiss public company)
agm	annual general meeting
APB	Accounting Principles Board
APC	Auditing Practices Committee (UK)
ASC	Accounting Standards Committee (UK)
CAPM	capital asset pricing model
CCA	current cost accounting
CGT	capital gains tax
COB	Commission des opérations de bourse (Stock Exchange Commission, France)
CONSOB	Commissione nazionale per le società e la borsa (Stock Exchange Commission, Italy)
CPA	certified public accountant
CPP	current purchasing power accounting
CTT	capital transfer tax
DCF	discounted cash flow
ecu	European currency unit
EEC	European Economic Community
EFT	electronic funds transfer
EOQ	economic order quantity
eps	earnings per share
FASB	Financial Accounting Standards Board (USA)
FCA	Fellow of the Institute of Chartered Accountants in England and Wales
FIFO	first in, first out
GAAP	generally accepted accounting principles
GmbH	Gesellschaft mit beschränkter Haftung (German or Swiss private company)
IRR	internal rate of return
IRS	Internal Revenue Service (USA)
LIFO	last in, first out
MCT	mainstream corporation tax
NPV	net present value
NRV	net realisable value

p/e	price/earnings ratio
P & L a/c	profit and loss account
plc	public limited company (UK)
PRT	petroleum revenue tax (UK)
R & D	research and development
ROCE	return on capital employed
ROI	return on investment
SA	société anonyme (French, Belgian, Luxembourg or Swiss public company)
sàrL	Société à responsabilité limitée (French, etc private company)
SEC	Securities and Exchange Commission (USA)
SIB	Securities and Investments Board
SSAP	Statement of Standard Accounting Practice (UK)
UEC	Union Européenne des Experts Comptables Economiques et Financiers
USM	Unlisted Securities Market (UK)
VAT	value added tax
ZBB	zero base budgeting

For international bodies and their abbreviations, see ORGANISATIONS.

-able, -eable, -ible.

-able	*-eable*	*-ible*
debatable	**manageable**	**convertible**
dispensable	**traceable**	**digestible**
disputable	**serviceable**	**inadmissible**
indescribable	**sizeable**	**indestructible**
indictable		**investible**
indistinguishable		**permissible**
livable		**submersible**
implacable		
ratable		
salable (but prefer **sellable**)		
unmistakable		
unshakable		

Accents. On words now accepted as English, use accents only when they make a crucial difference to pronunciation: **cliché, soupçon, façade, café, communiqué.**

If you use one accent, use all: **émigré, mêlée, protégé, résumé.**

Put the accents and cedillas on French names and words, and umlauts on German ones: **François Mitterrand, Klöckner.** Leave the accents off Spanish and other foreign names.

Accountancy ratios.
Working capital

Working capital ratio = current assets/current liabilities, where current assets = stock + debtors + cash at bank and in hand + quoted investments, etc, current liabilities = creditors + overdraft at bank + taxation + dividends, etc. The ratio varies according to type of trade and conditions; a ratio from 1 to 3 is usual with a ratio above 2 being generally good.

Liquidity ratio = liquid ("quick") assets/current liabilities, where liquid assets = debtors + cash at bank and in hand + quoted investments (that is assets which can be realised within a month or so, which may not apply to all investments); current liabilities are those which may need to be repaid within the same short period, which may not necessarily include a bank overdraft where it is likely to be renewed. The liquidity ratio is sometimes referred to as the "acid test"; a ratio under 1 suggests a possibly difficult situation, while too high a ratio may mean that assets are not being usefully employed.

Turnover of working capital = sales/average working capital. The ratio varies according to type of trade; generally a low ratio can mean poor use of resources, while too high a ratio can mean over-trading.

Turnover of stock = sales/average stock, or (where cost of sales is known) = cost of sales/average stock. The cost of sales turnover figure is to be preferred as both figures are then on the same valuation basis. This ratio can be expressed as number of times per year, or time taken for stock to be turned over once = (52/number of times) weeks. A low turnover of stock can be a sign of stocks which are difficult to move, and is usually a sign of adverse conditions.

Turnover of debtors = credit sales/average debtors. This indicates efficiency in collecting accounts. An average "credit period" of about 1 month is usual, but varies according to credit stringency conditions in the economy.

Turnover of creditors = purchases/average creditors. Average payment period is best maintained in line with turnover of debtors.

Sales

Export ratio = exports as a percentage of sales.

Sales per employee = sales/average number of employees.

Assets

Ratios of assets can vary according to the measure of assets used:

Total assets = current assets + fixed assets + other assets, where fixed assets = property + plant and machinery + motor vehicles, etc, and other assets = long-term investment + goodwill, etc.

Net assets ("net worth") = total assets − total liabilities
= share capital + reserves

Turnover of net assets = sales/average net assets. As for turnover of working capital, a low ratio can mean poor use of resources.

Assets per employee = assets/average number of employees. Indicates the amount of investment backing for employees.

Profits
Profit margin = (profit/sales) × 100 = profits as a percentage of sales; usually profits before tax.

Profitability = (profit/total assets) × 100 = profits as a percentage of total assets.

Return on capital = (profit/net assets) × 100 = profits as a percentage of net assets ("net worth" or "capital employed").

Active. Use active verbs, not passive ones. It is not incumbent on you to be pompous.

Adverbs. Put adverbs where you would put them in normal speech, which is usually after the verb (not before it, which usually is where Americans put them). Choose tenses according to British usage, too. In particular, do not fight shy – as Americans often do – of the perfect tense, especially where no date or time is given. Thus **Mr Reagan has woken up to the danger** is preferable to **Mr Reagan woke up to the danger**, unless you can add **last week** or **when he heard the explosion**.

Agree. Things are agreed **on, to** or **about**, not just agreed.

Aggression. Is a bad thing, so do not call a keen salesman an **aggressive** one (unless his foot is in the door – or beyond).

Alibi. An **alibi** is the fact of being elsewhere, not a false explanation.

Alternative. This is one of two, not one of three, four, five or more.

Americanisms. Do not use too many Americanisms. Many American words and expressions have passed into the language; others have vigour, particularly if used occasionally. Some are short and to the point (so prefer **lay off** to **make redundant**). But many are unnecessarily long (so use **and** not **additionally, car** not **automobile, company** not **corporation, transport** not **transportation, district** not **neighbourhood, oblige** not **obligate, stocks** not **inventories** unless there is the risk of confusion with stocks and shares). Other Americanisms are obscure or objectionable (so avoid **affirmative action, rookies, end runs, stand-offs, point men, ball games** and almost all American sporting terms). Do not write **meet with** or **outside of:** outside America you just **meet** people. Do not **figure out** if you can **work out. Cut** rather than **cut back.** And do not use such nouns as **author, critique, host, impact, loan, party, pressure** and **roundtable** as verbs.

Prefer **doctors** to **physicians** and **lawyers** to **attorneys.** They are to be found **in** Harley Street or Wall Street, not **on** it. And they rest from their labours **at** weekends, not **on** them.

In an American context you may **run** for office (but please **stand** in Britain), and your car may sometimes run on **gasoline** instead of **petrol.** But if you use **corn** in the American sense you should explain that this is **maize** to most people (unless it is an **old chestnut**). People in buses and trains are **passengers,** not **riders. Cars** are **hired,** not **rented. City centres** are not **central cities.** Cricket is a **game,** not a **sport.** London is the **country's** capital, not the **nation's. Ex-servicemen** are not necessarily **veterans.**

Make a **deep study** or even a **study in depth,** but not an **in-depth study.** Move **towards** not **toward.** Throw **stones,** not **rocks** – unless they are of **slate,** which can also mean **abuse** (as a verb), but does not, in English, mean **predict. Regular** is not a synonym for **ordinary** or **normal:** Mussolini brought in the **regular** train, All-Bran the **regular** man; it is quite **normal** to be without either. **Hikes** are walks, not **increases.** Vegetables, not teenagers, should be **fresh.** Only the speechless are **dumb. Scenarios** are best kept for the theatre, **postures** for the gym, **parameters** for the parabola.

You may **program** a computer but in all other contexts the word is **programme.**

Do not feel obliged to follow American fashion in overusing such words as **constituency** (try **supporters**), **perception** (try **belief** or **view**) and **rhetoric** (of which there is too little, not too much – try **language** or **speeches** or **grandiloquence** if that is what you mean). And if you must use American expressions, use them correctly (a **rain-check** does not imply checking on the shower activity). Above all, remember that many Americans read *The Economist* because they like to read good English. They do not want to read prose loaded with Americanisms. Nor do most other readers.

Ampersands. Ampersands should be used (1) when they are part of the name of a company (eg, AT&T, **Pratt & Whitney**); (2) for such things as constituencies where two names are linked to form one unit (eg, **The rest of Brighouse & Spenborough joins with the Batley part of Batley & Morley to form Batley & Spen**); (3) in R&D.

Anticipate. Does not mean **expect**. Jack and Jill expected to marry; **if they anticipated marriage, only Jill might find herself expectant.**

Apostrophes. Use the normal possessive ending **'s** after singular words or names that end in s: **caucus's, boss's, St James's, Jones's, Tindemans's**. Use it after plurals that do not end in s: **children's, Frenchmen's, media's**.

Use the ending **s'** on plurals that end in s – **Danes', bosses', Joneses'** – including plural names that take a singular verb, eg, **Reuters', Barclays', Stewarts & Lloyds', Salomon Brothers'**.

Although singular in other respects, the United States, the United Nations, the Philippines, etc, have a plural possessive apostrophe: eg, **What will the United States' next move be?**

People's = of (the) people.

Peoples' = of peoples.

Try to avoid using **Lloyd's** as a possessive; it poses an insoluble problem.

Appeal. Is intransitive nowadays (except in America), so **appeal against** decisions.

As of (April 5th or April). Do not use. Instead, write: **On** (or **after**, or **since**) April 5th, **in** April.

As to. There is usually a more appropriate preposition.

Autarchy means absolute sovereignty. **Autarky** means self-sufficiency.

B

Beaufort Scale. See WIND SPEED.

Black. In the black means **in profit** in Britain, but **making losses** in many other places. Always use **in profit**.

Blacks. See COUNTRIES.

Both . . . and. A preposition placed after **both** should be repeated after **and**, eg, **both to London and to Slough**; but **to both London and Slough** is all right.

Brackets. If a whole sentence is within brackets, put the full stop inside. Square brackets should be used for interpolations in direct quotations. Thus, **"Let them [the poor] eat cake."** To use ordinary curved brackets implies that the words inside them were part of the original text from which you are quoting.

C

Calendars. There are five important solar calendars.

Gregorian	Iranian[a]	Indian[b]
January (31)		
February (28 or 29)		
March (31)	Favardin (31)	Chaitra (30)
April (30)	Ordibehesht (31)	Vaisakha (31)
May (31)	Khordad (31)	Jyaistha (31)
June (30)	Tir (31)	Asadha (31)
July (31)	Mordad (31)	Sravana (31)
August (31)	Sharivar (31)	Bhadra (31)
September (30)	Mehr (30)	Asvina (30)
October (31)	Aban (30)	Kartika (30)
November (30)	Azar (30)	Agrahayana (30)
December (31)	Dey (30)	Pausa (30)
(January)	Bahman (30)	Magha (30)
(February)	Esfand (28 or 29)	Phalguna (30)

Gregorian	Ethiopian[c]	Hebrew[d]
September (30)	Maskerem (30)	Tishri (30)
October (31)	Tikimit (30)	Cheshvan (29 or 30)
November (30)	Hidar (30)	Kislev (29 or 30)
December (31)	Tahsas (30)	Tevet (29)
(January)	Tir (30)	Shevat (30)
(February)	Yekatit (30)	Adar (29)
(March)	Megabit (30)	Nissan (30)
(April)	Miazia (30)	Iyyar (29)
(May)	Guenbot (30)	Sivan (30)
(June)	Sene (30)	Tammuz (29)
(July)	Hamle (30)	Av (30)
(August)	Nahassie (30 + 5 or 6)	Ellul (29)

[a] Months begin about the 21st of the corresponding Gregorian month.
[b] Months begin about the 22nd of the corresponding Gregorian month.
[c] Months begin on the 11th of the corresponding Gregorian month.
[d] The date of the new year varies, but normally falls in the second half of September in the Gregorian calendar; the general calendar position is maintained by adding, in some years, an extra period of 11 days, Adar Sheni, following the month of Adar.

Figures in brackets denote the number of days in that month.

The Muslim calendar. Muslims use a lunar calendar which begins 10 or 11 days earlier each year in terms of the Gregorian. The months are as follows.

Muharram (30 days)	Rajab (30)
Saphar (29)	Shaaban (29)
Rabia I (30)	Ramadan (30)
Rabia II (29)	Shawwal (29)
Gamada I (30)	Dhulkaada (30)
Gamada II (29)	Dhulheggia (29 or 30)

In each 30 years, 19 years have 354 days (are "common") and 11 have 355 days (are "intercalary").

Muslim years begin on the following dates of the Gregorian calendar.

1407	September 6 1986
1408	August 26 1987
1409	August 14 1988
1410	August 4 1989
1411	July 24 1990
1412	July 13 1991
1413	July 2 1992

Canute's exercise on the sea-shore was designed to persuade his courtiers of what he knew to be true but they doubted, ie, that he was not omnipotent. Don't imply he was surprised to get his feet wet.

Capitals. A balance has to be struck between so many capitals that the eyes dance and so few that the reader is diverted more by our style than by our substance. The general rule is to dignify with capital letters ORGANISATIONS and institutions, but not people. More exact rules are laid out below. Even these, however, leave some decisions to individual judgment. If in doubt use lower case unless it looks absurd. And remember that "a foolish consistency is the hobgoblin of little minds" (Emerson). (See also ABBREVIATIONS.)

People. Use upper case for ranks and TITLES when written in conjunction with a name, but lower case when on their own, thus, **President Reagan**, but the **president; Vice-President Bush**, but the **vice-president; Colonel Qaddafi** but the **colonel**. Do not write **Prime Minister Thatcher** or **Chancellor Kohl**; she is **the prime minister, Mrs Thatcher**, he is **the federal chancellor, Mr Kohl**.

All office holders when referred to merely by their office, not by their name, are lower case: **the prime minister, the foreign secretary, the chancellor of the exchequer, the treasury secretary, the**

president of the United States, the chairman of the National Coal Board.

The only exceptions are (1) a few titles that would look unduly peculiar without capitals, eg, **Black Rod, Master of the Rolls, Chancellor of the Duchy of Lancaster, Lord Privy Seal, Lord Chancellor**; (2) a few exalted people: the **Queen** (Britain's only), the **Pope**, the **Shah** (historical references), **the Speaker** (to avoid confusion), the **Dalai Lama**, the **Aga Khan**. Also **God**.

Organisations, acts, etc. ORGANISATIONS, ministries, departments, treaties, acts, etc, generally take upper case when their full name (or something pretty close to it, eg, **State Department**) is used. Thus, **European Commission, Forestry Commission, Arab League, Amnesty International, the Household Cavalry, Ministry of Agriculture, Department of Trade, Treasury, Metropolitan Police, High Court, Supreme Court, Court of Appeal, Senate, Central Committee, Politburo, Oxford University, the London Stock Exchange, Treaty of Rome, the Health and Safety at Work Act**, etc.

So too the **House of Commons, House of Lords, House of Representatives** (each of which, after it has first been mentioned in full, may be referred to as **the House**), **St Paul's Cathedral** (**the cathedral**), **World Bank** (**the Bank**), **Bank of England** (**the Bank**), **Department of State** (**the department**).

But ORGANISATIONS, committees, commissions, special groups, etc, that are either impermanent, ad hoc, local or relatively insignificant should be lower case. Thus: **the subcommittee on entryism of the National Executive Committee of the Labour party, the international economic subcommittee of the Senate Foreign Relations Committee, the Oxford University bowls club, Market Blandings rural district council.**

Use lower case for rough descriptions (**the safety act,** the **American health department,** the **French parliament,** as distinct from its **National Assembly**). If you are not sure whether the English translation of a foreign name is exact or not, assume it is rough and use lower case.

Parliament and **Congress** are upper case. So, to avoid confusion, is the **Opposition** when used in the sense of **her majesty's loyal Opposition.** The **government, the administration** and the **cabinet** are always lower case.

The full name of political parties is upper case, except for the word party: **Social Democratic party** (abbreviated to SDP), **National party of Nigeria** (NPN). Note that only people are **Democrats** or **Social Democrats**; their parties, policies, committees, etc, are **Democratic** or **Social Democratic** (although a committee may be **Democrat-controlled**). The SDP–**Liberal Alliance** takes an uppercase a, even when it is referred to just as the **Alliance.**

When referring to a specific party, write **Labour,** the **Republican nominee,** a prominent **Liberal,** etc, but use lower case in looser references to **liberals, conservatism, communists,** etc. **Tories,** however, are upper case.

In finance and government there are some particular exceptions to the general rule of initial caps for full names, lower case for informal ones. Use caps for the **World Bank** and the **Fed** (after first spelling it out as the **Federal Reserve Board**) although these are shortened, informal names. The **Bank of England** and its foreign equivalents have initial caps when named formally and separately, but collectively they are central banks in lower case (except Ireland's, which is actually named the **Central Bank**). **Special drawing rights** are lower case but abbreviated in caps as SDRs.

After first mention, the **House of Commons** (or **Lords,** or **Representatives**) becomes the **House,** the **World Bank** and **Bank of England** become the **Bank** and the IMF can become the **Fund.** But most other organisations – agencies, banks, commissions (including the **European Commission**), etc – take lower case when referred to incompletely on second mention.

A political, economic or religious label formed from a proper name, eg, **Gaullism, Paisleyite, Leninist, Napoleonic, Wilsonian, Jacobite, Luddite, Marxist, Hobbesian, Bennery, Christian, Buddhism, Hindu, Maronite, Finlandisation,** should have a capital.

Places. Use upper case for definite geographical places, regions, areas and countries (eg, **The Hague, North-West Territories, West Germany, West Berlin**), and for vague but recognised political or geographical areas: **the Middle East, South Atlantic, East Asia** (which is to be preferred to **the Far East**), **the West** (as in **the decline of the West**), **the Gulf, North Atlantic, South-East Asia, the Midlands, Central America, the Highlands, the West Country, the South** (in the United States), **the Midwest, Western Europe.** But their adjectives can be lower case: **east-west relations, southern writers.** The **third world** is lower case.

If in doubt, use lower case (**the sunbelt**).

Use capitals for particular buildings, even if the name is not strictly accurate (eg, the **Foreign Office**).

Use lower case for province, county, state, city, when not strictly part of the name: **Washington state, Cabanas province, New York city.**

Use lower case for **east, west, north, south** except when part of a name (**East Berlin, South Africa, West End**), or when part of a thinking group: **the South** (in the United States), **the North-East** (of England).

Unpredictable political terms

Upper case	*Lower case*
Communist (a particular party)	**the crown**
Teamster	**white paper**
Warsaw Pact	**left**
The Speaker	**right**
	19th amendment
	communist (generally)
	constitution
	opposition
	civil service
	civil servant
	common market
	the ten

Historical periods: *upper case*

New Deal	**Middle Ages**
Reconstruction	**Black Death**
Renaissance	**Year of the Dog** (but new year and new
Restoration	year's day)
the Depression	

Trade names: *upper case*
Hoover, Valium, etc

Miscellaneous

Upper case	*Lower case*
Pershing missile (because it is named after somebody)	**cruise missile**
House of Laity	**the press**
Eurobond	**general synod**
the Davis Cup	**blacks**
the Cup Final	**aborigines**
the Bar	**new year**
Coloureds (in South Africa)	**new year's day**
Hispanics	**third world**
Catholics	
Protestants	

Cars. Here are some of the more familiar number plate abbreviations by country.

A	Austria	GB	Britain
AL	Albania	GR	Greece
AND	Andorra	I	Italy
B	Belgium	IRL	Ireland
BG	Bulgaria	L	Luxembourg
CH	Switzerland	NL	Holland
CS	Czechoslovakia	P	Portugal
D	West Germany	RO	Romania
DDR	East Germany	T	Turkey
DK	Denmark	USA	United States
E	Spain	YU	Yugoslavia
F	France		

Cassandra's predictions were correct but not believed.

Centred on, not **around** or **in.**

Charge. If you **charge** intransitively, do so as a bull, cavalry officer or somesuch, not as an **accuser** (so avoid: **The standard of writing was abysmal, he charged**).

Chinese names. In general follow the Pinyin spelling of Chinese names, which has replaced the old Wade-Giles system, except for people from the past, people and places outside mainland China, and for a few well-known places in mainland China. **Mao**, however, is **Zedong**, not **Tse-tung**. There are no hyphens in Pinyin spelling. So:

Pinyin	*Wade-Giles*
Deng Xiaoping	**Tse-tung**
Jiang Qing (ex-Mrs Mao)	**Chiang Kai-shek**
Hu Yaobang	**Peking** (not Beijing)
Mao Zedong	**Canton**
Wu Xueqian	**Shanghai**
Zhao Ziyang	**Hongkong**
Xinjiang (ex-Sinkiang)	
Guangdong (ex-Kwangtung)	
Tianjin (ex-Tientsin)	
Qingdao (ex-Tsingtao)	

The family name in China comes first, therefore **Deng Xiaoping** becomes **Mr Deng** on a later mention (pronounced **dung**).

Names from **Singapore, Korea, Vietnam** – no hyphens:
Lee Kuan Yew
Ho Chi Minh.

Circumstances stand around a thing, so it is **in**, not **under**, them.

Cities. Correct spellings of the world's 100 biggest cities are listed here. (Some other problem spellings are listed under PLACES.)

1	Mexico City	Mexico	25	Guangzhou	China
2	São Paulo	Brazil	26	Istanbul	Turkey
3	Shanghai	China	27	Leningrad	Soviet Union
4	Tokyo	Japan	28	Philadelphia	United States
5	Buenos Aires	Argentina	29	Lima	Peru
6	Peking	China	30	Tehran	Iran
7	Calcutta	India	31	Shenyang	China
8	New York	United States	32	Detroit	United States
9	Rio de Janeiro	Brazil	33	Bogota	Colombia
10	Paris	France	34	Madras	India
11	Moscow	Soviet Union	35	Luda	China
12	Seoul	South Korea	36	Santiago	Chile
13	Bombay	India	37	Wuhan	China
14	Tianjin	China	38	Dhaka	Bangladesh
15	Los Angeles	United States	39	Ho Chi Minh	Vietnam
16	Chicago	United States	40	Baghdad	Iraq
17	London	Britain	41	Sydney	Australia
18	Jakarta	Indonesia	42	San Francisco	United States
19	Chongqing	China	43	Nanjing	China
20	Manila	Philippines	44	Ankara	Turkey
21	Delhi	India	45	Madrid	Spain
22	Bangkok	Thailand	46	Pusan	South Korea
23	Karachi	Pakistan	47	Washington	United States
24	Cairo	Egypt	48	Athens	Greece

49	Toronto	Canada	75	Rangoon	Burma
50	Dallas	United States	76	Taipei	Taiwan
51	Lahore	Pakistan	77	Pittsburgh	United States
52	Bangalore	India	78	Porto Alegre	Brazil
53	Houston	United States	79	Baltimore	United States
54	Caracas	Venezuela	80	Bucharest	Romania
55	Rome	Italy	81	Minneapolis	United States
56	Montreal	Canada	82=	Harbin	China
57	Yokohama	Japan	82=	Lagos	Nigeria
58	Melbourne	Australia	84	Nagoya	Japan
59	Boston	United States	85	Budapest	Hungary
60	Osaka	Japan	86	Monterrey	Mexico
61	Nassau County	United States	87	Atlanta	United States
62	Hanoi	Vietnam	88	Surabaja	Indonesia
63	Belo Horizonte	Brazil	89=	Chengdu	China
64	Hyderabad	India	89=	Lanzhou	China
65	Ahmedabad	India	91	Izmir	Turkey
66	Guadalajara	Mexico	92	Newark	United States
67	Singapore	Singapore	93	Tashkent	Soviet Union
68	Kowloon	Hongkong	94	Anaheim	United States
69	Kinshasa	Zaire	95	Havana	Cuba
70	Casablanca	Morocco	96	Cleveland	United States
71	St Louis	United States	97	West Berlin	West Germany
72	Kiev	Soviet Union	98	San Diego	United States
73	Recife	Brazil	99=	Ch'ang-ch'un	China
74	Alexandria	Egypt	99=	Taiyuan	China

Collective nouns. There is no firm rule about the number of a verb governed by a singular collective noun. It is best to go by the sense – ie, whether the collective noun stands for a single entity. (**The council was elected in March, The army is on a voluntary basis**) or for its constituents (**The council are at sixes and sevens over rates, The army are above the average civilian height**).

A safe rule for **number: The number is . . ., A number are . . .**

A **government**, a **party**, a **company** (whether Tesco or Marks and Spencer) and a **partnership** (Skidmore, Owings & Merrill) are all **it** and take a singular verb. So does a **country**, even if its name looks plural. Thus **The United States is helping the Philippines.** The **United Nations** is singular. **Politics** is also singular; so is **economics**.

Brokers too. **Vickers da Costa is preparing a statement.** Avoid **stockbrokers Vickers da Costa, bankers Chase Manhattan** or **accountants Peat, Marwick.**

Colons. Use a colon "to deliver the goods that have been invoiced in the preceding words" (Fowler). **They brought presents: gold, frankincense and oil at $35 a barrel.**

Use a colon before a whole quoted sentence, but not before a quotation that begins in mid-sentence. **She said: "It will never work." He retorted that it had "always worked before".**

Use a colon for antithesis or "gnomic contrasts" (Fowler). **Man proposes: God disposes.**

See also SEMICOLONS.

Come up with. Try **suggest** or **produce** instead.

Commas. Use commas as an aid to understanding. Too many in one sentence can be confusing.

Use two commas, or none at all, when inserting a clause in the middle of a sentence. Thus, do not write: **Use two commas, or none at all when inserting . . .** or **Use two commas or none at all, when inserting . . .**

But, in 1968, students revolted; not **But in 1968, students revolted.**

If the clause ends with a bracket, which is not uncommon (this one does), the bracket should be followed by a comma.

Do not put a comma before **and** at the end of a sequence of items unless one of the items includes another **and**. Thus: **its main exports were tobacco, asbestos, meat and copper.** But: **Its main exports were tobacco, asbestos, meat and hides, and copper.**

Commas are useful to break up a long sentence, but should be used only where the break is a natural one. Do not insert or remove commas unnecessarily on proofs.

Commas in DATES: none.

Commodities and manufactured goods. Most countries use the Standard International Trade Classification to describe the goods they import and trade. A list of the main items follows.

There are 9 sections, giving single digits 1 to 9; divisions within these sections have 2-digit numbers and groups within each division have 3-digit numbers. In the list below all sections and divisions are shown, together with selected groups. There are also 4-digit subgroups in the full SITC list, with, for example, 072.3 for "cocoa butter and cocoa paste" as a subgroup of 072 ("cocoa"), and further breakdowns for some items into a 5-digit level, with, for example, 072.32 for "cocoa butter (fat or oil)".

Throughout, nes stands for "not elsewhere specified".

0	Food and live animals
00	Live animals
01	Meat and meat preparations
02	Dairy products and birds' eggs
022	Milk and cream
023	Butter
024	Cheese and curd
03	Fish, crustaceans and molluscs, and preparations thereof
04	Cereals and cereal preparations
041	Wheat (including spelt) and meslin, unmilled
042	Rice
043	Barley, unmilled
044	Maize (corn), unmilled
05	Vegetables and fruit
06	Sugar, sugar preparations and honey
07	Coffee, tea, cocoa, spices and manufactures thereof
071	Coffee and coffee substitutes
072	Cocoa
074	Tea and maté
08	Feeding stuff for animals (not including unmilled cereals)
09	Miscellaneous edible products and preparations
1	Beverages and tobacco
11	Beverages
112	Alcoholic beverages
12	Tobacco and tobacco manufactures
2	Crude materials, inedible, except fuels
21	Hides, skins and furskins, raw
22	Oil seeds and oleaginous fruit
23	Crude rubber (including synthetic and reclaimed)
24	Cork and wood
25	Pulp and waste paper

26	Textile fibres (other than wool tops), and their wastes (not manufactured into yarn or fabric)
263	Cotton
266	Synthetic fibres suitable for spinning
267	Other man-made fibres suitable for spinning and waste of man-made fibres
268	Wool and other animal hair (excluding wool tops)
27	Crude fertilisers and crude minerals (excluding coal, petroleum and precious stones)
28	Metalliferous ores and metal scrap
281	Iron ore and concentrates
29	Crude animal and vegetable materials, nes
3	Mineral fuels, lubricants and related materials
32	Coal, coke, and briquettes
33	Petroleum, petroleum products and related materials
333	Petroleum oils, crude, and crude oils obtained from bituminous materials
334	Petroleum products, refined
34	Gas, natural and manufactured
35	Electric current
4	Animal and vegetable oils, fats and waxes
41	Animal oils and fats
42	Fixed vegetable oils and fats
43	Animal and vegetable oils and fats, processed, and waxes of animal or vegetable origin
5	Chemical and related products, nes
51	Organic chemicals
52	Inorganic chemicals
53	Dyeing, tanning and colouring materials
54	Medicinal and pharmaceutical products
55	Essential oils and perfume materials; toilet, polishing and cleansing preparations
56	Fertilisers, manufactured
57	Explosives and pyrotechnic products
58	Artificial resins and plastic materials, and cellulose esters and ethers
59	Chemical materials and products, nes
6	Manufactured goods, classified chiefly by material
61	Leather, leather manufactures, nes and dressed furskins
62	Rubber manufactures, nes
63	Cork and wood manufactures (excluding furniture)
64	Paper, paperboard and articles of paper pulp, of paper or of paperboard

65	Textile yarn, fabrics, made-up articles, nes, and related products
66	Non-metallic mineral manufactures, nes
67	Iron and steel
68	Non-ferrous metals
681	Silver, platinum and other metals of the platinum group
682	Copper
683	Nickel
684	Aluminium
687	Tin
69	Manufactures of metal, nes
7	Machinery and transport equipment
71	Power generating machinery and equipment
713	Internal combustion piston engines, and parts thereof, nes
72	Machinery specialised for particular industries
721	Agricultural machinery (excluding tractors) and parts thereof, nes
724	Textile and leather machinery, and parts thereof, nes
73	Metalworking machinery
74	General industrial machinery and equipment, nes, and machine parts, nes
75	Office machines and automatic data processing equipment
76	Telecommunications and sound recording and reproducing apparatus and equipment
761	Television receivers (including receivers incorporating radio-broadcast receivers or sound recorders or reproducers)
77	Electrical machinery, apparatus and appliances, nes, and electrical parts thereof (including non-electrical counterparts, nes, of electrical household type equipment)
78	Road vehicles (including air-cushion vehicles)
781	Passenger motor cars (other than public-service type vehicles), including vehicles designed for the transport of both passengers and goods
782	Motor vehicles for the transport of goods or materials and special purpose motor vehicles
79	Other transport equipment
791	Railway vehicles (including hovertrains) and associated equipment
792	Aircraft and associated equipment, and parts thereof, nes
793	Ships, boats (including hovercraft) and floating structures
8	Miscellaneous manufactured articles
81	Sanitary, plumbing, heating and lighting fixtures and fittings, nes

82	Furniture and parts thereof
83	Travel goods, handbags and similar containers
84	Articles of apparel and clothing accessories
85	Footwear
87	Professional, scientific and controlling instruments and apparatus, nes
88	Photographic apparatus, equipment and supplies and optical goods, nes; watches and clocks
881	Photographic apparatus and equipment, nes
885	Watches and clocks
89	Miscellaneous manufactured articles, nes
9	Commodities and transactions not classified elsewhere in the SITC
911.0	Postal packages not classified according to kind
931.0	Special transactions and commodities not classified according to kind
941.0	Animals, live, nes (including zoo animals, dogs, cats, insects, etc)
951.0	Armoured fighting vehicles, arms of war and ammunition therefor, and parts of arms, nes
961.0	Coin (other than gold coin), not being legal tender
971.0	Gold, non-monetary (excluding gold ores and concentrates)

Companies. Call companies by the names they call themselves (impossible typographical flourishes excluded).

Here are some confusing ones.

B.A.T Industries
Chesebrough-Pond's
Lloyds (the bank)
Lloyd's (the insurance market)
Marks and Spencer plc
Marks & Spencer (name above the shop)
Salomon Brothers

Some other British company names are listed under STOCK MARKET INDICES.

Crawford's Directory of City Connections (The Economist Publications, London) lists most big British companies, and makes a point of spelling their names using each one's preferred style.

Company abbreviations. The table on page 22 gives abbreviated designations for various types of companies.

Abbreviated company names

	Private	Public
America	--------Inc, Ltd --------	
Britain	Ltd	plc
France	Sàrl	SA
W. Germany	GmbH	AG
Holland	BV	NV
Italy	Srl	SpA

Compare. A is compared **with B** when you draw attention to the difference. A is compared **to B** only when you want to stress their similarity (**Shall I compare thee to a summer's day?**).

Compound does not mean make worse. To **compound a felony** means to **agree for a consideration not to prosecute**; intransitively, to compound means to **agree** or **come to terms**.

Comprise means **is composed of. The Democratic coalition comprises women, workers, blacks and Jews. Women make up** (not comprise) **three–fifths of the Democratic coalition.** Alternatively, **Three–fifths of the Democratic coalition is composed of women.**

Convince. Don't use it if you mean **persuade. The prime minister was persuaded to call a June election; she was convinced of the wisdom of doing so only after she had won.**

Countries and currencies

Countries (and their inhabitants). In most contexts sacrifice precision to simplicity and use **Britain** rather than **Great Britain** or the **United Kingdom, America** rather than the **United States,** and **Holland** rather than the **Netherlands.** The **Soviet Union** can sometimes be called **Russia,** though the full name is generally better. Inaccuracy also triumphs over ugliness, so call the inhabitants of the Soviet Union **Russians,** not Soviets.

It is sometimes important, however, to be precise, in which case remember that **Great Britain** consists of **England, Scotland** and **Wales,** which together with **Northern Ireland** (which we generally called **Ulster,** though Ulster strictly includes three counties in the republic of **Ireland**), make up the **United Kingdom.**

Remember, too, that although it is usually all right to talk about the inhabitants of the United States as **Americans,** the term also applies to everyone from Canada to Cape Horn. It may sometimes be necessary to write **United States** (never US) **citizens.**

When writing about Spanish-speaking people in the United States, use either **Latino** or **Hispanic** as a general term but try to be specific (eg, Mexican-American).

Africans may be black or white. If you mean blacks, write **blacks**.

Currencies. Use **$** as the standard currency and in general convert currencies to **$** on first mention.

Britain
1p 2p 3p to **99p** (not £0.99)
£6 (not £6.00)
£5,000–6,000 (not £5,000–£6,000)
£5m–6m (not £5m–£6m)

£5 billion–6 billion (not £5–6 billion)

A **billion** is a thousand million, a **trillion** is a thousand billion.

America
$** will do generally, but write **US$ if other kinds of dollars are being used in the same text.

Spell out **cents**.

A$, C$, HK$, M$, NZ$** and **S$ are Australian, Canadian, Hong-kong, Malaysian, New Zealand and Singapore $ or dollars. Other currencies are **DM, BFr, FFr, SFr, IR£** (punts), **ASch, Ptas, R, SDR, DKr** (Danish krone, kroner), **NKr** (Norwegian krone, kroner), **SKr** (Swedish krona, kronor), **Y** and **Rmb** (Chinese renminbi, not yuan).

With all these, the practice is to write the abbreviation followed by the figure: **Y100** (not 100 yen), **R100** (not 100 rand), **SDR1m** (not 1m SDRs). Sums in other currencies, including the **ecu**, are written in full, with the number first: **100m ecus, 100m escudos, 100m guilders, 100m kwacha, 100m lire** (if Italian, **liras** if Turkish), **100m naira, 100m pesos, 100m rupees.**

Note: currencies are not set in small caps.

A full list of currencies and countries follows. (Currency symbols are included for reference, not necessarily for use.)

Country	Currency	Symbol
Abu Dhabi	UAE dirham	Dh
Afghanistan	afghani	Af
Albania	lek	Lk
Algeria	Algerian dinar	AD
America	dollar	$
Angola	kwanza	Kz
Argentina	austral	A
Australia	Australian dollar	A$
Austria	schilling	ASch
Bahamas	Bahamian dollar	B$
Bahrain	Bahrain dinar	BD
Bangladesh	taka	Tk
Barbados	Barbadian dollar	Bd$
Belgium	Belgian franc	BFr
Belize	Belizean dollar	Bz$
Benin	CFA franc	CFAfr
Bermuda	Bermuda dollar	Bda$
Bolivia	Bolivian peso	peso
Botswana	pula	P
Brazil	cruzado	Cz
Britain	pound/sterling	£
Brunei	Brunei dollar	Br$
Bulgaria	lev	Lv
Burkina Faso	CFA franc	CFAfr
Burma	kyat	Kt
Burundi	Burundi franc	Bufr
Cambodia	riel	CRl
Cameroon	CFA franc	CFAfr
Canada	Canadian dollar	C$
Cape Verde Islands	Cape Verde escudo	CVEsc
Central African Republic	CFA franc	CFAfr
Chad	CFA franc	CFAfr
Chile	Chilean peso	peso
China	renminbi	Rmb
Colombia	Colombian peso	peso
Comoros	Comoran franc	Cfr
Congo	CFA franc	CFAfr
Costa Rica	Costa Rican colón	¢
Cuba	Cuban peso	peso
Cyprus	Cyprus pound/Turkish lira	C£/TL
Czechoslovakia	koruna	Kcs
Denmark	Danish krone	DKr
Djibouti	Djibouti franc	Dfr
Dominican Republic	Dominican Republic peso	peso
Dubai	UAE dirham	Dh
East Germany	mark	Em

Country	Currency	Symbol
Ecuador	sucre	Su
Egypt	Egyptian pound	£E
El Salvador	El Salvador colón	¢
Equatorial Guinea	CFA franc	CFAfr
Ethiopia	birr	Birr
European currency unit	ecu	ecu
Fiji	Fiji dollar	F$
Finland	markka	Fmk
France	franc	FFr
Gabon	CFA franc	CFAfr
Gambia, The	dalasi	D
Ghana	cedi	₡
Greece	drachma	Dr
Guatemala	quetzal	Q
Guinea	syli	GS
Guinea-Bissau	Guinea-Bissau peso	P
Guyana	Guyanese dollar	G$
Haiti	gourde	Gourde
Holland	guilder	G or Fl
Honduras	lempira	La
Hongkong	Hongkong dollar	HK$
Hungary	forint	Ft
Iceland	Iceland new krona	Ikr
India	Indian rupee	Rs
Indonesia	rupiah	Rp
Iran	rial	IR
Iraq	Iraqi dinar	ID
Ireland	punt	IR£
Israel	shekel	IS
Italy	lira	L
Ivory Coast	CFA franc	CFAfr
Jamaica	Jamaican dollar	J$
Japan	yen	¥
Jordan	Jordan dinar	JD
Kenya	Kenya shilling	KSh
Kuwait	Kuwaiti dinar	KD
Laos	kip	K
Lebanon	Lebanese pound	L£
Lesotho	maloti	M
Liberia	Liberian dollar	L$
Libya	Libyan dinar	LD
Luxembourg	Luxembourg franc	Luxfr
Macau	pataca	MPtc
Madagascar	Madagascar franc	Mgfr
Malawi	kwacha	K
Malaysia	Malaysian dollar/Ringgit	M$

Country	Currency	Symbol
Mali	CFA franc	CFAfr
Malta	Maltese lira	Lm
Mauritania	ouguiya	UM
Mauritius	Mauritius rupee	MRs
Mexico	Mexican peso	peso
Morocco	dirham	Dh
Mozambique	metical	MT
Namibia	South African rand	R
Nepal	Nepalese rupee	NRs
Netherlands Antilles	Netherlands Antilles guilder	NAG
New Zealand	New Zealand dollar	NZ$
Nicaragua	córdoba	C
Niger	CFA franc	CFAfr
Nigeria	naira	₦
North Korea	won	Won
North Yemen	Yemeni rial	YR
Norway	Norwegian krone	NKr
Oman	Omani rial	OR
Pakistan	Pakistan rupee	PRs
Panama	balboa	B
Papua New Guinea	Kina	Kina
Paraguay	guarani	₲
Peru	sol	sol
Philippines	Philippine peso	P
Poland	zloty	Zl
Portugal	escudo	Esc
Puerto Rico	US dollar	$
Qatar	Qatari riyal	QR
Romania	leu	Lei
Rwanda	Rwandan franc	Rwfr
São Tomé & Príncipe	dobra	Db
Saudi Arabia	Saudi riyal	SR
Senegal	CFA franc	CFAfr
Seychelles	Seychelles rupee	SRs
Sierra Leone	leone	Le
Singapore	Singapore dollar	S$
Solomon Islands	Solomon Island dollar	SI$
Somalia	Somali shilling	SoSh
South Africa	rand	R
South Korea	won	W
South Yemen	Yemeni dinar	YD
Soviet Union	rouble	Rb
Spain	peseta	Pta
Sri Lanka	Sri Lanka rupee	SLRs
Sudan	Sudanese pound	S£

Country	Currency	Symbol
Surinam	Surinam guilder	SG
Swaziland	emalengeni	E
Sweden	Swedish krona	Skr
Switzerland	Swiss franc	SFr
Syria	Syrian pound	S£
Taiwan	New Taiwan dollar	NT$
Tanzania	Tanzanian shilling	TSh
Thailand	baht	Bt
Togo	CFA franc	CFAfr
Tonga	Tonga dollar	T$
Trinidad & Tobago	TT dollar	TT$
Tunisia	Tunisian dinar	TD
Turkey	Turkish lira	TL
Uganda	Ugandan shilling	USh
United Arab Emirates	UAE dirham	Dh
Uruguay	Uruguayan new peso	peso
Vanuatu	vatu	Vt
Venezuela	bolivar	Bs
Vietnam	dong	D
West Germany	mark	DM
Western Samoa	Tala	Tala
Windward & Leeward Isles	East Caribbean dollar	EC$
Yugoslavia	Yugoslav dinar	YuD
Zaire	zaire	Z
Zambia	kwacha	K
Zimbabwe	Zimbabwe dollar	Z$

D

Dashes. You can use dashes in pairs for parenthesis, but not more than one pair per sentence, ideally not more than one pair per paragraph.

Use a dash to introduce an explanation, amplification, paraphrase, particularisation or correction of what immediately precedes it.

Use it to gather up the subject of a long sentence.

Use it to introduce a paradoxical or whimsical ending to a sentence.

Do not use it as a punctuation maid-of-all-work (Gowers).

Dates. Do not put commas in dates, so:
July 5th
Monday July 5th   *better as July 5th.*
July 5 1987 (no th)   *or*
July 5–12 1987   *5 July*
July 12–August 5 1987
July 1987
1987–88 *(NB 1987/88)*
1980s

Write out:
twentieth century
twentieth-century ideas,
but
a man in his 20s, and 20th anniversary.

In general give dates; **last week** or **last month** can cause confusion.
But WWII Write **the second world war** or **the 1939–45 war**, not **world war**
& standard **II**; similarly, prefer **the first world war** to **world war I. Postwar** and **prewar** are not hyphenated.

See also CALENDARS.

Decimals. See FRACTIONS.

Decimate means to destroy a proportion (originally a tenth) of a group of people or things, not to destroy them all or nearly all.

Different from, not **to** or **than.**

Disinterested means impartial; **uninterested** means bored.

Due to = (1) owed to, as in: **£1 is due to Smith**; (2) arranged or timed to, as in: the **meeting is due to end on Friday**; (3) because of. When used in this sense, it must follow a noun, as in **the cancellation, due to rain, of . . .** Do not write **It was cancelled due to rain.**
Better to avoid, or use 'because of'.

E

Earnings. Do not write **earnings** when you mean **profits** (say if they are operating, gross, pre-tax or net).

Earthquakes. The Richter scale defines the magnitude of an earthquake in terms of the energy released.

Richter Scale	Joules	Explosion equivalent TNT terms	Nuclear terms
0[a]	7.9×10^2	175 mg	
1	6.0×10^4	13 g	
2	4.0×10^6	0.89 kg	
3	2.4×10^8	53 kg	
4	1.3×10^{10}	3 tons	
5[b]	6.3×10^{11}	140 tons	
6[c]	2.7×10^{13}	6 kilotons	1/3 atomic bomb
7	1.1×10^{15}	240 kilotons	12 atomic bombs
8	3.7×10^{16}	8.25 megatons	1/3 hydrogen bomb
9	1.1×10^{18}	250 megatons	13 hydrogen bombs
10	3.2×10^{19}	7000 megatons	350 hydrogen bombs

[a] Approximately equal to the shock caused by an average man jumping from a table.
[b] Potentially damaging to structures.
[c] Potentially capable of general destruction; widespread damage is usually caused above magnitude 6.5.
Note: One atomic bomb is equivalent to 6.3 on the Richter scale, and one hydrogen bomb to 8.2.

Here are some examples.

	Richter scale
Mexico City, 1986	7.8
San Francisco, 1906	8.3
Chile, 1960	8.3
Krakatoa, 1883	9.9 (estimate)

Effectively means **with effect**; if you mean **in effect**, say it. **The matter was effectively dealt with on Friday** means it was well done on Friday. **The matter was, in effect, dealt with on Friday** means it was more or less attended to on Friday.

Elements. These are the natural and artificially created elements.

Name	Symbol	Name	Symbol
Actinium	Ac	Iodine	I
Aluminium	Al	Iridium	Ir
Americium	Am	Iron	Fe
Antimony (Stibium)	Sb	Krypton	Kr
Argon	Ar	Lanthanum	La
Arsenic	As	Lawrencium	Lr
Astatine	At	Lead	Pb
Barium	Ba	Lithium	Li
Berkelium	Bk	Lutetium	Lu
Beryllium	Be	Magnesium	Mg
Bismuth	Bi	Manganese	Mn
Boron	B	Mendelevium	Md
Bromine	Br	Mercury	Hg
Cadmium	Cd	Molybdenum	Mo
Caesium	Cs	Neodymium	Nd
Calcium	Ca	Neon	Ne
Californium	Cf	Neptunium	Np
Carbon	C	Nickel	Ni
Cerium	Ce	Niobium	Nb
Chlorine	Cl	Nitrogen	N
Chromium	Cr	Nobelium	No
Cobalt	Co	Osmium	Os
Copper	Cu	Oxygen	O
Curium	Cm	Palladium	Pd
Dysprosium	Dy	Phosphorus	P
Einsteinium	Es	Platinum	Pt
Erbium	Er	Plutonium	Pu
Europium	Eu	Polonium	Po
Fermium	Fm	Potassium (Kalium)	K
Fluorine	F	Praseodymium	Pr
Francium	Fr	Promethium	Pm
Gadolinium	Gd	Protactinium	Pa
Gallium	Ga	Radium	Ra
Germanium	Ge	Radon	Rn
Gold	Au	Rhenium	Re
Hafnium	Hf	Rhodium	Rh
Helium	He	Rubidium	Rb
Holmium	Ho	Ruthenium	Ru
Hydrogen	H	Samarium	Sm
Indium	In	Scandium	Sc

Name	Symbol	Name	Symbol
Selenium	Se	Titanium	Ti
Silicon	Si	Tungsten	*see Wolfram*
Silver	Ag	Unnilhexium[c]	Unh[c]
Sodium (Natrium)	Na	Unnilpentium[c]	Unp[c]
Strontium	Sr	Unnilquadium[c]	Unq[c]
Sulphur	S	Uranium	U
Tantalum	Ta	Vanadium	V
Technetium	Tc	Wolfram	W
Tellurium	Te	Xenon	Xe
Terbium	Tb	Ytterbium	Yb
Thallium	Tl	Yttrium	Y
Thorium	Th	Zinc	Zn
Thulium	Tm	Zirconium	Zr
Tin	Sn		

Estimated. Avoid **an estimated 300 casualties**; prefer **about 300** or **it was estimated that there were 300**.

Ex., Be careful with **ex: a Liberal ex-member** has lost his seat; **an ex-Liberal member** has lost his party.

F

Fewer (not less) **than seven speeches, fewer than seven samurai.**
Use **fewer**, not **less**, with numbers of individual items or people.
Less than £200, less than 700 tonnes of oil, because these are
measured quantities, not individual items.

Figures. Never start a sentence with a figure; write the number in
words instead.

Use figures for numerals from 11 upwards, and for all numerals
that include a decimal point or a fraction (eg, **4.25, 4¼**). Use words for
simple numerals from one to ten, except: in references to pages; in
percentages (eg, **4%**); and in sets of numerals, eg, **Deaths from this
cause in the past three years were 14, 9 and 6.**

Do not compare a fraction with a decimal (so avoid **The rate fell
from 3½% to 3.1%**). To convert one to the other, see FRACTIONS.

FRACTIONS should be hyphenated (**two-thirds, five-eighths**, etc).

Use **m** for **million,** but spell out **billion** – which to us means
1,000m – except in charts, where **bn** is permissible. Thus: **8m, £8m, 8
billion, DM8 billion.** You may use either **2½m** or **2.5m,** but do not
mix decimals and fractions.

Use **5,000–6,000, 5–6%, 5m–6m** (not **5-6m**) and **5 billion–6
billion.** But **sales rose from 5m to 6m** (not **5m–6m**); **estimates
ranged between 5m and 6m** (not **5m–6m**).

Where **to** is being used as part of a ratio, it is usually best to spell it
out. Thus **They decided, by nine votes to two, to put the matter
to the general assembly which voted, 27 to 19, to insist that the
ratio of vodka to tomato juice in a bloody mary should be at
least one to three, though the odds of this being so in most bars
were put at no better than 11 to 4.** Where the ratio is being used
adjectivally, figures and hyphens may be used, but only if one of the
figures is greater than ten: thus **a 50–20 vote, a 19–9 vote.** Otherwise,
spell out the figures and use **to: a two-to-one vote, a ten-to-one
likelihood.**

With figures, use **a head** or **per cent, a year** or **per year,** not **per
caput, per capita** or **per annum. Kilowatt, milliwatt** and
megawatt, meaning **1,000 watts, one thousandth of a watt** and
1m watts, are abbreviated to **kW, mW** and **MW.** See MEASURES.

In general prefer **acres** to **hectares, miles** to **kilometres, yards** to
metres, etc; if using **hectares,** you should give an equivalent in **acres**
or **square miles.**

The style for aircraft types can be confusing. Some have hyphens in
obvious places (eg, DC-10, **Mirage** F-1E, MIG-21), some in unusual places
(BAC 1-11) and some none at all (BAe 146, **TriStar**). Others have both
name and number (**Lockheed** P-3 **Orion**). When in doubt, use "Jane's
All The World's Aircraft". Its index also includes manufacturers'
correct names.

The style for calibres is 50mm or 105mm with no hyphen, but 5.5-inch and 25-pounder.

Finally. Do not use this word when, at the end of a series, you mean **lastly** or, in other contexts, when you mean **at last**. To write **The Dow finally fell below 1200** is absurd because it may rise past 1200.

Flaunt means display; **flout** means disdain. If you flout this distinction you will flaunt your ignorance.

Foreign words and phrases. Try not to use them unless there is no English alternative, which is unusual (so **a year** or **per year**, not **per annum; a head** or **per head**, not **per caput, per capita**, etc).

Forgo means **do without**; it forgoes the e. **Forego** means **go before**.

Former. Avoid wherever possible use of **the former** and **the latter**. It causes confusion.

Fractions. Do not mingle fractions with decimals. If you need to convert one to the other, use this table.

Fraction	Decimal equivalent
1/2	0.5
1/3	0.333
1/4	0.25
1/5	0.2
1/6	0.167
1/7	0.143
1/8	0.125
1/9	0.111
1/10	0.1
1/11	0.091
1/12	0.083
1/13	0.077
1/14	0.071
1/15	0.067
1/16	0.063

Full stops. Use plenty. They keep sentences short. This helps the reader.

Do not use full stops in ABBREVIATIONS or at the end of headings.

G

Gender is a word to be applied to grammar, not people. If someone is female, that is her **sex** not her gender.

Geological eras. Astronomers and geologists give this broad outline of the ages of the universe and the earth.

Era, period and epoch	Years ago (year at beginning)	Characteristics
Origin of the universe (estimates vary markedly)	20,000,000,000 to 10,000,000,000	
Origin of the sun	5,000,000,000	
Origin of the earth	4,600,000,000	
Precambrian		
Archean	4,000,000,000	First signs of fossilised microbes
Proterozoic	2,500,000,000	
Palaeozoic		
Cambrian	600,000,000	First appearance of abundant fossils
Ordovician (obsolete)	500,000,000	Vertebrates emerge
Silurian	440,000,000	Fishes emerge
Devonian	400,000,000	Primitive plants emerge
Carboniferous	350,000,000	Amphibians emerge
Permian	290,000,000	Reptiles emerge
Mesozoic		
Triassic	250,000,000	Seed plants emerge
Jurassic	210,000,000	Age of dinosaurs
Cretaceous	145,000,000	Flowering plants emerge; dinosaurs extinct at end of this period

Era, period and epoch	Years ago (year at beginning)	Characteristics
Cenozoic		
Palaeocene	65,000,000	
Tertiary: Eocene	55,000,000	Mammals emerge
Oligocene	40,000,000	
Miocene	25,000,000	
Pliocene	5,000,000	
Quaternary:		
Pleistocene	2,000,000	Ice ages; stone age man emerges
Holocene or Recent	10,000	Modern man emerges

Get. An adaptable verb, but it has its limits. A man does not get sacked or promoted; he is sacked or promoted.

H

Healthy. If you think something is **desirable** or **good**, say so. Do not call it healthy.

Hobson's choice is not the lesser of two evils; it is no choice at all.

Hopefully. By all means begin an article hopefully, but never write: **Hopefully, it will be finished by Monday.** Try: **With luck, if all goes well, it is hoped that . . .**

Hyphens. Use hyphens in the following words.
1) FRACTIONS (whether nouns or adjectives): **two-thirds, four-fifths,** etc.
2) Most words that begin with **anti, non** and **neo:** Thus, **anti-fascist, anti-submarine** (but **anticlimax, antidote, antiseptic, antitrust**); **non-combatant, non-existent, non-payment, non-violent** (but **nonaligned, nonconformist, nonplussed, nonstop**); **neo-conservative.**
3) A sum followed by the word **worth** also needs a hyphen. Thus **$25m-worth of goods.**
4) Some titles:

	but
vice-president	
director-general	**general secretary**
under-secretary	**deputy secretary**
secretary-general	**deputy director**
attorney-general	**district attorney**

5) To avoid ambiguities:
a little-used car
a little used-car
cross complaint
cross-complaint
high-school girl
high schoolgirl
fine-tooth comb (most people do not comb their teeth)
6) Aircraft:
DC-10
Mirage F-1E
MIG-23
Lockheed P-3 **Orion**
(If in doubt, consult "Jane's All the World's Aircraft".)
7) Adjectives formed from two or more words:
right-wing groups (but **the right wing** of the party)
balance-of-payments difficulties
private-sector wages

public-sector borrowing requirement
a 70-year-old judge
value-added tax (VAT)

But do not overdo the literary device of hyphenating words that are not usually linked: the stringing-together-of-lots-and-lots-of-words-and-ideas tendency can be tiresome.

8) Separating identical letters: **book-keeping** (but **bookseller**), **coat-tails, co-operate, unco-operative, pre-eminent, pre-empt** (but **predate, precondition**), **re-emerge, re-entry** (but **rearrange, reborn, repurchase**), **trans-ship**.

9) Nouns formed from prepositional verbs: **build-up, call-up, get-together, round-up, set-up, shake-up**, etc.

10) The quarters of the compass: **north-east(ern), south-east(ern), south-west(ern), north-west(ern)**, but the **Midwest**.

11) No hyphens: **carmaker, carworker, steelmaker, steelworker** are single words. But in other industries use two words with no hyphens (so **metal worker, tyre maker, coal miner**).

One word

airfield	**prewar**
businessman	**profitmaking**
bypass	**seabed**
carmaker	**shipbuilding**
carworker	**shipbuilders**
ceasefire	**soyabean**
comeback	**steelmaker**
commonsense (adj)	**steelworker**
forever	**stockmarket**
halfhearted	**subcommittee**
handout	**subcontinent**
handpicked	**subhuman**
lacklustre	**submachinegun**
machinegun	**sunbelt**
nevertheless	**takeover**
nonetheless	**underdog**
offshore	**underpaid**
onshore	**wartime**
overpaid	**videodisc**
override	**videocassette**
petrochemical	**workforce**
policymaker, policymaking	**worldwide**
postwar	**worthwhile**

Two words	*Three words*
air base	**capital gains tax**
air force	**foreign policy maker**
aircraft carrier	**in as much**
ballot box	**in so far**
chip maker	
coal miner	
common sense (noun)	
errand boy	
girl friend	
microchip maker	
on to	
place name	
strong man	
under way	
well known	

12) For hyphens in names see SPELLING.

13) Dates: avoid **from 1947–50** (say **in 1947–50** or **from 1947 to 1950**) and **between 1961–65** (say **in 1961–65** or **from 1961 to 1965**).

I

Important. If something is important say why and to whom.

Initials. Initials in people's names, or in companies named after them, take points. Thus, **Mr I. F. Stone, Mr P. W. Botha, W. H. Smith, F. W. Woolworth.** (The only exceptions are for people or companies who deliberately leave them out; in general, follow the practice preferred by both people and companies in writing their own names.)

Inverted commas (quotes). Use single ones only for quotations within quotations. Thus: **"When I say 'immediately', I mean some time before April,"** said the spokesman.

When a quotation is indented and set in smaller type than the main bodymatter, do not put inverted commas on it. (Indented copy should usually go down 1pt. The new para after an indent is always full out.)

For the relative placing of quotation marks and punctuation, follow Hart's rules. If an extract ends with a full stop or question-mark, put the punctuation before the closing inverted commas. An example from Hart:

"The passing crowd" is a phrase coined in the spirit of indifference. Yet, to a man of what Plato calls "universal sympathies", and even to the plain, ordinary denizens of this world, what can be more interesting than those who constitute "the passing crowd"?

When a quotation is broken off and resumed after such words as **he said**, ask yourself whether it would naturally have had any punctuation at the point where it is broken off. If the answer is yes, a comma is placed within the quotation marks to represent this. Thus, **"It cannot be done," he said; "we must give up the task."** The comma after **done** belongs to the quotation and so comes within the inverted commas, as does the final full stop.

But if the words to be quoted are continuous, without punctuation at the point where they are broken, the comma should be outside the inverted commas. Thus:

"Go home", he said, "to your father."

If a complete sentence in quotes comes at the end of a larger sentence, the final stop should be inside the inverted commas. Thus:

He said curtly, "It cannot be done."

Italics. Use for:

1) Foreign words and phrases, such as *cabinet* (French type), *apparentement, Mitbestimmung, tolkach*, unless they are so familiar that they have become anglicised. (Thus **ad hoc, machismo, putsch, pogrom, status quo**, etc, are in roman). Make sure that the meaning of any foreign word you use is clear.

2) Newspapers and periodicals. Note that only *The Economist* and *The Times* have their *The* italicised. Thus the *Daily Telegraph*, the *New York Times*, the *Observer*, the *Spectator* etc (but *Le Monde, Die Welt, Die Zeit*). Books, pamphlets, plays, radio and television programmes are roman, with capital letters for each main word, in quotation marks. Thus: "Pride and Prejudice", "Much Ado about Nothing", "Any Questions", "Face the Nation" etc.

3) Lawsuits. Thus: *Brown v Board of Education. Coatsworth v Johnson.* If abbreviated, *versus* should always be shortened to *v*, with no point after it.

4) The names of ships, aircraft, spacecraft. Thus: HMS *Illustrious, Spirit of St Louis, Challenger*, etc.

Note that a ship is "**she**".

Do not use italics in titles or captions.

J

Jargon. Avoid it. All sections of *The Economist* should be intelligible to all our readers, most of whom are foreigners. You may have to think harder if you are not to use jargon, but you can still be precise.

Technical terms should be used in their proper context; do not use them out of it. There are simple words which can usually do the job of **exponential** (try **fast**), **interface** (**frontier**) and so on. To **fund** is a technical term, meaning to convert floating debt into more or less permanent debt at fixed interest; do not use it if you mean to **finance**, or to **pay for**.

Avoid, above all, meaningless or ambiguous jargon, such as **15% more fuel-efficient**.

K

Key. Keys may be **major** or **minor**, but not **low**. Few of the decisions, people, industries described as **key** are truly indispensable.

L

Last. (1) **The last issue of** *The Economist* implies our extinction; prefer **last week's issue, the previous issue.** Likewise avoid **the last issue of** *Foreign Affairs*: prefer the **latest, current,** or (eg) **June issue,** or **this month's** or **last month's issue.** (2) **Last year,** in 1985, means 1984: if you mean the 12 months up to the time of writing, write **the past year.** The same goes for the **past** month, **past** week, **past** (not **last**) 10 years.

Laws. Scientific, economic, facetious and fatalistic laws in common use are listed here.

Boyle's Law. The pressure of a gas varies inversely with its volume at constant temperature.

Gresham's Law. When money of a high intrinsic value is in circulation with money of lesser value, it is the inferior currency which tends to remain in circulation, while the other is either hoarded or exported. In other words: "Bad money drives out good".

Grimm's Law. (Concerns mutations of the consonants in the various Germanic languages.) Proto-Indo-European voiced aspirated stops, voiced unaspirated stops and voiceless stops become voiced unaspirated stops, voiceless stops and voiceless fricatives respectively.

Heisenberg's Uncertainty Principle. Energy and time or position and momentum cannot both be accurately measured simultaneously. The product of their uncertainties is always greater than or equal to $h/4\pi$, where h is the Planck constant.

Hooke's Law. The stress imposed on a solid is directly proportional to the strain produced within the elastic limit.

Mendel's Principles. The Law of Segregation is that every somatic cell of an individual carries a pair of hereditary units for each character: the pairs separate during meiosis so that each gamete carries only one unit of each pair.

The Law of Independent Assortment is that the separation of units of each pair is not influenced by that of any other pair.

Murphy's Law. Anything that can go wrong will go wrong.

Ohm's Law. Electric current is directly proportional to electromotive force and inversely proportional to resistance.

Parkinson's Law. First published in *The Economist*, November 19 1955. The author, C. Northcote Parkinson, sought to expand on the "commonplace observation that work expands so as to fill the time available for its completion". After studying Admiralty staffing levels, he concluded: In any public administrative department not actually at war the staff increase may be expected to follow this formula:

$$x = \frac{2k^m + p}{n}$$

Where k is the number of staff seeking promotion through the appointment of subordinates; p represents the difference between the ages of appointment and retirement; m is the number of man-hours devoted to answering minutes within the department; and n is the number of effective units being administered. Then x will be the number of new staff required each year.

Mathematicians will, of course, realise that to find the percentage increase they must multiply x by 100 and divide by the total of the previous year, thus:

$$\frac{100(2k^m + p)}{yn} \%$$

where y represents the total original staff. And this figure will invariably prove to be between 5.17 per cent and 6.56 per cent, irrespective of any variation in the amount of work (if any) to be done.

The Peter Principle. All members of a hierarchy rise to their own level of incompetence.

Say's Law of Markets. A supply of goods generates a demand for the goods.

Laws of Thermodynamics
1) The change in the internal energy of a system equals the sum of the heat added to the system and the work done on it.
2) Heat cannot be transferred from a colder to a hotter body within a system without net changes occurring in other bodies in the system.
3) It is impossible to reduce the temperature of a system to absolute zero in a finite number of steps.

Utz's laws of computer programming. Any given program, when running, is obsolete. If a program is useful, it will have to be changed. Any given program will expand to fill all available memory.

Wolfe's Law of Journalism. You cannot hope/to bribe or twist,/ thank God! the/British journalist./But, seeing what/the man will do/ unbribed, there's/no occasion to.

Leeway is leeward drift, not space to do a bit of manoeuvring in.

Lifestyle. Prefer **way of life**.

Light-year. A light-year is a measurement of distance, not of time. It is the approximate distance travelled by light in one year.
Thus:

$$1 \text{ light-year} = 5.88 \times 10^{12} \text{ miles}$$
$$= 9.46 \times 10^{12} \text{ km}$$

Lower case. See CAPITALS.

M

Manufactured goods. For a list of the main international classifications, see COMMODITIES AND MANUFACTURED GOODS.

Measures.

> **Rough conversions.** For British, American and metric (SI) measures. Metric units not generally recommended as SI units or for use with SI are marked with an asterisk (eg Calorie*).

Length
Width of thumb = 1 inch = 25 millimetres
1	inch	=	$2\frac{1}{2}$	centimetres
2	inches	=	5	centimetres
1	foot	=	30	centimetres = $\frac{1}{3}$ metre
$3\frac{1}{4}$	feet	=	1	metre
39	inches	=	1	metre
11	yards	=	10	metres
$\frac{5}{8}$	mile	=	1	kilometre
5	miles	=	8	kilometres
8	miles	=	7	nautical miles (international)

Area
1	square inch	=	$6\frac{1}{2}$	square centimetres
2	square inches	=	13	square centimetres
$10\frac{3}{4}$	square feet	=	1	square metre
43	square feet	=	4	square metres
6	square yards	=	5	square metres
$2\frac{1}{2}$	acres	=	1	hectare
5	acres	=	2	hectares
250	acres	=	1	square kilometre
3	square miles	=	8	square kilometres

Volume and capacity
1	teaspoonful	=	5	millilitres
1	UK fluid ounce	=	28	millilitres
26	UK fluid ounces	=	25	US liquid ounces
3	cubic inches	=	49	cubic centimetres
		=	49	millilitres
$1\frac{3}{4}$	UK pints	=	1	litre
7	UK pints	=	4	litres
7	UK quarts	=	8	litres
5	UK pints	=	6	US liquid pints
19	US liquid pints	=	9	litres
1	UK gallon	=	$4\frac{1}{2}$	litres
2	UK gallons	=	9	litres

5	UK gallons	= 6	US gallons
1	US gallon	=	$3\frac{3}{4}$ litres
4	US gallons	= 15	litres
3	cubic feet	= 85	cubic decimetres
		= 85	litres
35	cubic feet	= 1	cubic metre
4	cubic yards	= 3	cubic metres
31	UK bushels	= 32	US bushels
$27\frac{1}{2}$	UK bushels	= 1	cubic metre
$28\frac{1}{3}$	US bushels	= 1	cubic metre
11	UK bushels	= 4	hectolitres
14	US bushels	= 5	hectolitres
1	US bushel (heaped)	=	$1\frac{1}{4}$ US bushels (struck)
1	US dry barrel	=	$3\frac{1}{4}$ US bushels
1	US cranberry barrel	=	$2\frac{3}{4}$ US bushels
1	barrel (petroleum)	= 42	US gallons = 35 UK gallons
1	barrel per day	= 50	tonnes per year

Yield

3 UK or US bushels per acre	=	2 quintals★ per hectare
10 UK or US bushels per acre	=	9 hectolitres per hectare
1 UK hundredweight per acre	=	$1\frac{1}{4}$ quintals★ per hectare
1 UK ton per acre	=	$2\frac{1}{2}$ tonnes per hectare
9 pounds per acre	=	10 kilograms per hectare

Weight (mass)

1 grain	=	65 milligrams
$15\frac{1}{2}$ grains	=	1 gram
11 ounces	=	10 ounces troy
1 ounce	=	28 grams
1 ounce troy	=	31 grams
1 pound	=	454 grams
35 ounces	=	1 kilogram
$2\frac{1}{4}$ pounds	=	1 kilogram
11 stones	=	70 kilograms
11 US hundredweights	=	5 quintals★
2 UK hundredweights	=	1 quintal★
2205 pounds	=	1 tonne
11 US tons	=	10 tonnes
62 UK tons	=	63 tonnes
100 UK (long) tons	=	112 US (short) tons

Velocity (speed)

2 miles per hour	=	3 feet per second
9 miles per hour	=	4 metres per second

18 kilometres per hour =   5 metres per second
11 kilometres per hour = 10 feet per second
30 miles per hour   =   48 kilometres per hour
50 miles per hour   =   80 kilometres per hour
70 miles per hour   = 113 kilometres per hour

Fuel consumption
 5 UK gallons per mile = 14 litres per kilometre
20 miles per UK gallon = 7 kilometres per litre
20 miles per UK gallon = 14 litres per 100 kilometres
 5 miles per US gallon = 6 miles per UK gallon

Acceleration
Standard gravity = 10 metres per second squared
              = 32 feet per second squared

Density and concentration
 4 ounces per UK gallon = 25 grams per litre
 2 ounces per US gallon = 15 grams per litre
 1 pound per cubic foot = 16 kilograms per cubic metre
$62\frac{1}{2}$ pounds per cubic foot = 1 kilogram per litre
                    = density of 1

Force
$7\frac{1}{4}$ poundals   = 1 newton
1 pound-force   = $4\frac{1}{2}$ newtons
9 pounds-force   = 40 newtons
1 kilogram-force = 10 newtons

Pressure and stress
   1 pound-force per square foot = 48 pascals (newtons per square metre)
   1 pound-force per square inch = 7 kilopascals (kilonewtons per square metre)
   1 bar   = 1 standard atmosphere
                            = $14\frac{1}{2}$ pounds-force per square inch
100 pounds-force per square inch = 7 kilograms-force per square centimetre

Energy
18 British thermal units   = 19 kilojoules
 4 British thermal units   = 1 kilocalorie★
 1 kilocalorie★ ("Calorie"★) = 4 kilojoules

Power
 4 UK horsepower = 3 kilowatts
72 UK horsepower = 73 metric horsepower★

Here are the metric system prefixes.

Prefix name & symbol		Factor by which the unit is multiplied	Description
atto	a	10^{-18} = 0.000 000 000 000 000 001	
femto	f	10^{-15} = 0.000 000 000 000 001	
pico	p	10^{-12} = 0.000 000 000 001	one trillionth
nano	n	10^{-9} = 0.000 000 001	one billionth
micro	μ	10^{-6} = 0.000 001	one millionth
milli	m	10^{-3} = 0.001	one thousandth
centi	c	10^{-2} = 0.01	one hundredth
deci	d	10^{-1} = 0.1	one tenth
deca (or deka)	da[a]	10^{1} = 10	ten
ecto	h	10^{2} = 100	one hundred
kilo	k	10^{3} = 1,000	one thousand
myria	my	10^{4} = 10,000	ten thousand
mega	M	10^{6} = 1,000,000	one million
giga	G	10^{9} = 1,000,000,000	one thous.[b] m[c]; bn[d]
tera	T	10^{12} = 1,000,000,000,000	one m[c] m; trillion
peta	P	10^{15} = 1,000,000,000,000,000	
exa	E	10^{18} = 1,000,000,000,000,000,000	

[a] Sometimes dk is used (eg in West Germany).
[b] Thousand.
[c] Million.
[d] Billion.

Units with different equivalents
Barrel
a. United Kingdom (beer)   = 36 UK gallons = 164 litres
b. United States: dry standard   = 7,056 cubic inches = 116 litres
          petroleum   = 42 US gallons = 159 litres
          standard cranberry = 5,826 cubic inches = 95.5 litres
          various (liquid)   = 31–42 US gallons, 117–51 litres

Bushel
a. United Kingdom = 2,219.36 cubic inches = 36.37 litres
b. Old English, Winchester⎫
   United States[a] (struck[b]) ⎬ = 2,150.42 cubic inches = 35.24 litres
c. United States (heaped[c]) = 2,747.715 cubic inches = 45.03 litres

[a] The most usual unit. [b] Levelled off at the top. [c] Used for apples.

Centner or Zentner
a. United Kingdom = cental of 100 pounds = 45.36 kilograms
b. Commercial hundredweight in several European countries, generally 50 kilograms = 110.23 pounds
c. Metric centner of 100 kilograms = 220.46 pounds

Chain
a. United Kingdom: Gunter's surveyors'} = 66 feet = 20.12 metres
b. Engineers' = 100 feet = 30.48 metres

Foot
a. United Kingdom United States customary} = 12 inches = 0.304 8 metre
b. United States survey = 12.000 02 inches = 0.304 800 6 metre
c. Canada: Paris foot = 12.789 inches = 0.325 metre
d. Cape foot = 12.396 inches = 0.315 metre
e. Chinese foot (che or chih):
   old system = 14.1 inches = 0.358 metre
   new system = 13.123 inches = 0.333 33 metre

Gallon
a. United Kingdom = 277.42 cubic inches = 4.546 litres
b. Old English, Winchester, Wine United States, liquid} = 231 cubic inches = 3.785 litres
c. United States, dry = 268.802 5 cubic inches = 0.004 4 cubic metre

Gill
a. United Kingdom = 8.669 cubic inches = 142.1 millilitres
b. United States = 7.218 75 cubic inches = 118.3 millilitres

Hundredweight
a. United Kingdom United States, long} = 112 pounds = 50.8 kilograms
b. United States, short = 100 pounds = 45.4 kilograms

Link
a. United Kingdom: Gunter's surveyors'} = 0.66 foot = 0.201 2 metre
b. Engineers' = 1 foot = 0.304 8 metre

Mile
a. United Kingdom:
   imperial = 5,280 feet = 1.609 344 kilometres
   geographical = 6,080 feet = 1.853 184 kilometres
   nautical   (in practice sometimes 6,000 feet = 1.828 8
   sea   kilometres)

b. United States = 5,280 feet = 1.609 344 kilometres
c. International nautical = 1,852 metres = 6,076.12 feet

Ounce
a. Dry: ounce = 437½ grains = 28.35 grams
    ounce troy = 480 grains = 31.10 grams
b. Liquid or fluid ounce:
    i. United Kingdom = 1.734 cubic inches = 28.4 millilitres
       (20 fluid ounces = 1 pint)
    ii. United States = 1.805 cubic inches = 29.6 millilitres
        (16 liquid ounces = 1 liquid pint)

Peck
a. United Kingdom = 554.839 cubic inches = 9.092 cubic decimetres
   (litres)
b. United States = 537.605 cubic inches = 8.810 cubic decimetres
   (litres)

Pint
a. United Kingdom = 34.677 4 cubic inches = 0.568 litre
b. United States:
    i. dry = 33.600 312 5 cubic inches = 0.551 cubic decimetre (litre)
    ii. liquid = 28.875 cubic inches = 0.473 litre

Pound
a. United Kingdom ⎫
   United States ⎬ avoirdupois pound = 0.454 kilogram
b. United States: troy pound = 0.373 kilogram = 0.823 pound
   (avoirdupois)
c. Spanish (libra) = 0.460 kilogram = 1.014 pounds (avoirdupois)
d. 'Amsterdam' = 0.494 kilogram = 1.089 pounds (avoirdupois)
e. Danish (pund) = 0.5 kilogram = 1.102 pounds (avoirdupois)
f. Française (livre) = 0.490 kilogram = 1.079 pounds (avoirdupois)

Quart
a. United Kingdom = 69.355 cubic inches = 1.137 litres
b. United States:
    i. dry = 67.200 625 cubic inches = 1.101 cubic decimetres (litres)
    ii. liquid = 57.75 cubic inches = 0.946 litre

Quarter
United Kingdom:
a. Capacity = 8 bushels = 64 gallons = 2.909 hectolitres = 0.290 9
   cubic metre
b. Weight (mass) = 28 pounds = 12.701 kilograms
c. Cloth = 9 inches = 22.86 centimetres
d. Wines and spirits = 27½ to 30 gallons = 125 to 136 litres

Quintal
a. Hundredweight: United Kingdom = 112 pounds = 50.8 kilograms
                    United States = 100 pounds = 45.4 kilograms
b. Metric quintal = 100 kilograms = 220.46 pounds
c. Spanish quintal = 46 kilograms = 101.4 pounds

Stone
United Kingdom:
a. Imperial = 14 pounds = 6.350 kilograms
b. Smithfield = 8 pounds = 3.629 kilograms

Ton
a. United Kingdom:
    i. weight (mass) = 2,240 pounds = 1.016 tonnes
    ii. shipping: register = 100 cubic feet = 2.832 cubic metres
b. United States:
    i. short = 2,000 pounds = 0.907 tonne
    ii. long = 2,240 pounds = 1.016 tonnes
c. Metric ton (tonne) = 1,000 kilograms = 2,204.62 pounds
d. Spanish:
    i. short (corta) = 2,000 libras = 0.920 2 tonne = 2,028.7 pounds
    ii. long (larga) = 2,240 libras = 1.030 6 tonnes = 2,272.1 pounds

Metaphors. "A newly invented metaphor assists thought by evoking a visual image," said Orwell, "while on the other hand a metaphor which is technically 'dead' (eg, **iron resolution**) has in effect reverted to being an ordinary word and can generally be used without loss of vividness. But in between these two classes there is a huge dump of wornout metaphors which are merely used because they save people the trouble of inventing phrases for themselves."

A single issue of *The Economist* contained these examples: **snail's pace, stem the deluge, wage explosion, put on ice, booms and busts, nest eggs, a question-mark hangs over inflation, patch together a compromise, breathe a sigh of relief, package, bonanza, hot favourite, whopping, up for grabs, pillars of the ruling party, low-profile leader, shining example.** Most of these are tired, and will therefore tire the reader. Some are so exhausted that they may be considered dead, and are therefore permissible. But use all metaphors – dead or alive – sparingly, otherwise you will make trouble for yourself.

The same issue of *The Economist* had a "committee of inquiry **stretching every nerve** to make its recommendations sufficiently inflationary for Britain's water strikers to accept them; and all who participated as **flag-wavers** in this surrender . . . have created a **whirlpool** of new public-sector inflation". Further on: "The market for remote-sensing data will need careful **nursing** if it is to **flower** into a commercial **bonanza** in the 1990s. Therein **lies the rub.**" Then: "The 1981 export **boom** has now **fed** through into the current account, bringing it into balance . . . Falling oil prices this year stand to **swing** it into a big surplus." And "It is a nasty **blow** to those private companies who, **egged on** by the government, borrowed dollars in the **halcyon** days when bankers **dished out** money to anything Brazilian."

More horrible still was a story which, beneath the heading "The EEC **plays its China card**", began: "The EEC **hit back** this week with a Chinese **tit** for America's Egyptian **tat.** Miffed at seeing the Americans **snatch** a 1m-tonne wheat flour deal with Egypt **from under their noses** last month, the community has **lined up** a cheap wheat sale of over 1m tonnes to China." The next paragraph opened by saying: "The **groundwork** for the China deal was laid during a **bargain-hunting** visit to Brussels . . ." Two paragraphs later it was asserted that "although the community **seized on** the China deal . . . as a way of giving the Americans **a little of their own medicine,** there is no **stomach** in Brussels for an all-out export subsidy **war** with the United States". It was no surprise that by the end of this, the fourth, paragraph, the author was "**not cutting much ice**".

Mete. You may **mete** out punishment, but if it is to fit the crime it is **meet.**

Metric system. See MEASURES.

Move. Do not use if you mean **decision, bid, deal** or something more precise. But **move** rather than **relocate.**

N

Names. See CHINESE NAMES, PEOPLE, SPELLING.

National Accounts. These are the definitions adopted by the United Nations in 1968.

Final expenditure
=   private final consumption expenditure ("consumers' expenditure")
+ government final consumption expenditure
+ increase in stocks
+ gross fixed capital formation
+ exports of goods and services

Gross domestic product at market prices
=   final expenditure
− imports of goods and services

Gross national product at market prices
=   gross domestic product at market prices
+ net property income from other countries

Gross domestic product at factor cost
=   gross domestic product at market prices
− indirect taxes
+ subsidies

Neither, nor. See NONE.

None usually takes a singular verb. So does **neither A nor B . . .**, unless B is plural, as in **neither the Dutchman nor the Danes have done it**, where the verb agrees with the element closest to it.

O

Olympic Games.

1896	Athens	1944	London (cancelled)
1900	Paris	1948	London
1904	St Louis	1952	Helsinki
1906	Athens	1956	Melbourne
1908	London	1960	Rome
1912	Stockholm	1964	Tokyo
1916	Berlin (cancelled)	1968	Mexico City
1920	Antwerp	1972	Munich
1924	Paris	1976	Montreal
1928	Amsterdam	1980	Moscow
1932	Los Angeles	1984	Los Angeles
1936	Berlin	1988	Seoul
1940	Tokyo/Helsinki (cancelled)		

Only. Put **only** as close as you can to the words it qualifies, eg, **these animals mate only in June**; to say that **they only mate in June** implies that in June they do nothing else.

Organisations. These are the exact names and abbreviated titles of the main international organisations. Where membership is small or exclusive, members are listed too.

ASEAN. Association of South East Asian Nations.

Members
Brunei   Indonesia   Malaysia   Philippines   Singapore   Thailand

Observer: Papua New Guinea.

BIS. Bank for International Settlements. The central bankers' central bank, in Basle. Its members are the Group of Ten, plus Switzerland.

Caricom. Caribbean Community and Common Market.

Members

Antigua and Barbuda	Guyana
Bahamas	Jamaica
Barbados	Montserrat
Belize	St Kitts-Nevis
Dominica	St Vincent and the Grenadines
Granada	Trinidad and Tobago

Observers: Dominican Republic, Haiti, Surinam.

Comecon. The Council for Mutual Economic Assistance, the communist world's version of the EUROPEAN ECONOMIC COMMUNITY.

Members

Bulgaria	Poland
Cuba	Romania
Czechoslovakia	Soviet Union
East Germany	Vietnam
Hungary	

Commonwealth

Members

Antigua and Barbuda	Mauritius
Australia	Nauru[a]
Bahamas	New Zealand
Bangladesh	Nigeria
Barbados	Papua New Guinea
Belize	St Kitts-Nevis
Botswana	St Lucia
Brunei	St Vincent and the Grenadines[a]
Canada	Seychelles
Cyprus	Sierra Leone
Dominica	Singapore
Fiji	Solomon Islands
The Gambia	Sri Lanka
Ghana	Swaziland
Grenada	Tanzania
Guyana	Tonga
India	Trinidad and Tobago
Jamaica	Tuvalu[a]
Kenya	Uganda
Kiribati	United Kingdom
Lesotho	Vanuatu
Malawi	Western Samoa
Malaysia	Zambia
Maldives[a]	Zimbabwe
Malta	

[a] Do not attend Commonwealth summits.

Dependencies and associated states
Australia:
   Australian Antarctic Territory
   Christmas Island
   Cocos (Keeling) Islands

Coral Sea Islands Territory
Heard and McDonald Islands
Norfolk Island
New Zealand:
  Cook Islands
  Niue
  Ross Dependency
  Tokelau
United Kingdom:
  Anguilla
  Bermuda
  British Antarctic Territory
  British Indian Ocean Territory
  British Virgin Islands
  Cayman Islands
  Channel Islands
  Falkland Islands
  Falkland Islands Dependencies
  Gibraltar
  Hongkong
  Isle of Man
  Montserrat
  Pitcairn Islands
  St Helena-Ascension, Tristan da Cunha
  Turks and Caicos Islands

ECOWAS. Economic Community of West African States.

Members

Benin	Liberia
Burkina Faso	Mali
Cape Verde	Mauritania
The Gambia	Niger
Ghana	Nigeria
Guinea	Senegal
Guinea-Bissau	Sierra Leone
Ivory Coast	Togo

EEC. European Economic Community, part of the European Communities, which also include the European Coal and Steel Community (ECSC) and the European Atomic Energy Community (Euratom).

Members
Belgium   Britain   Denmark   France   West Germany   Holland
Greece   Ireland   Italy   Luxembourg   Portugal   Spain

Franc Zone. Comité Monétaire de la Zone Franc.

Members

Benin[a]	French Republic[c]
Burkina Faso[a]	Gabon[b]
Cameroon[b]	Ivory Coast[a]
Central African Republic[c]	Mali[a]
Chad[b]	Niger[a]
Comoros[b]	Senegal[a]
Congo[b]	Togo[a]
Equatorial Guinea[b]	

[a] Member of Banque Centrale des Etats de l'Afrique de l'Ouest.
[b] Member of Banque des Etats de l'Afrique Centrale.
[c] Metropolitan France, Mayotte and the Overseas Departments and Territories.

Francophonie. French speaking equivalent of the Commonwealth, set up at the Francophone Summit in February 1986. At the meeting were the governments of:

Belgium	Laos
Benin	Lebanon
Burkina Faso	Luxembourg
Burundi	Madagascar
Cameroon	Mali
Canada	Mauritania
Central African Republic	Mauritius
Chad	Monaco
Comoros	Morocco
Congo	Niger
Djibouti	Rwanda
Dominica	St Lucia
Egypt	Senegal
France	Seychelles
Gabon	Togo
Guinea	Tunisia
Guinea-Bissau	Vanuatu
Haiti	Vietnam
Ivory Coast	Zaire

There were also delegations from: Communauté Français de Belgique Louisiana New Brunswick Quebec

GCC. Co-operation Council for the Arab States of the Gulf. Its normal shorthand name is Gulf Co-operation Council.

Members
Bahrain Kuwait Oman Qatar Saudi Arabia
United Arab Emirates

Group of Five. A subset of the Group of Ten, it consists of the finance ministries and central bank governors of Britain, France, West Germany, America and Japan. Occasional, purportedly secret meetings. The G-5 is a forum for influencing exchange rates and discussing IMF and World Bank policy.

Group of Ten. The ten leading countries – America, Britain, West Germany, France, Belgium, Holland, Italy, Sweden, Canada and Japan and an honorary eleventh member, Switzerland – that agreed to provide credit of $6 billion to the International Monetary Fund in 1962, known as the General Arrangement to Borrow. The G-10 is a convenient forum for discussing international monetary arrangements; it hatched up the Smithsonian agreement and currency changes in 1971. The G-10 also meets through its central bank, the Bank for International Settlements (BIS), based in Basle.

IATA. International Air Transport Association. Head offices: Montreal and Geneva. Members: most international airlines.

ICFTU. International Confederation of Free Trade Unions. Links trade unions from the political right wing and centre. Based in Brussels.

NATO. North Atlantic Treaty Organisation.

Members
Belgium
Britain
Canada
Denmark
France (withdrew from the integrated military structure in 1966 but remains a member of the Atlantic Alliance)
West Germany
Greece
Holland
Iceland
Italy
Luxembourg
Norway
Portugal
Spain
Turkey
United States of America

OAU. Organisation of African Unity.

Members

Algeria	Libya
Angola	Madagascar
Benin	Malawi
Botswana	Mali
Burkina Faso	Mauritania
Burundi	Mauritius
Cameroon	Morocco
Cape Verde	Mozambique
Central African Republic	Niger
Chad	Nigeria
Comoros	Rwanda
Congo	São Tomé and Príncipe
Djibouti	Senegal
Egypt	Seychelles
Equatorial Guinea	Sierra Leone
Ethiopia	Somalia
Gabon	Sudan
The Gambia	Swaziland
Ghana	Tanzania
Guinea	Togo
Guinea-Bissau	Tunisia
Ivory Coast	Uganda
Kenya	Zaire
Lesotho	Zambia
Liberia	Zimbabwe

The Sahara Arab Democratic Republic (Western Sahara) was admitted in February 1982, following recognition by 26 of the 50 members, but its membership was disputed by Morocco and others which claimed that 2/3 majority was needed to admit a state whose existence is in question.

OAS. Organization of American States.

Members

Antigua and Barbuda	Costa Rica
Argentina	Cuba
Bahamas	Dominica
Barbados	Dominican Republic
Bolivia	Ecuador
Brazil	El Salvador
Chile	Grenada
Colombia	Guatemala

Haiti	St Kitts-Nevis
Honduras	St Lucia
Jamaica	St Vincent and the Grenadines
Mexico	Surinam
Nicaragua	Trinidad and Tobago
Panama	United States of America
Paraguay	Uruguay
Peru	Venezuela

OECD. Organisation for Economic Co-operation and Development. Capitalism's club, based in Paris.

Members

Australia	Italy
Austria	Japan
Belgium	Luxembourg
Canada	New Zealand
Denmark	Norway
Finland	Portugal
France	Spain
West Germany	Sweden
Greece	Switzerland
Holland	Turkey
Iceland	United Kingdom
Ireland	United States of America

Yugoslavia has a special status, halfway between observer and participant.

SEATO. South-east Asia Treaty Organisation (disbanded 1977).

Members
United States of America   Australia   Britain   France   New Zealand
Pakistan   Philippines   Thailand

The United Nations. New York.

United Nations Regional Economic Commissions	*Head office*
Economic Commission for Europe – ECE	Geneva
Economic and Social Commission for Asia and the Pacific – ESCAP	Bangkok
Economic Commission for Latin America and the Caribbean – ECLA	Santiago, Chile
Economic Commission for Africa – ECA	Addis Ababa
Economic Commission for Western Asia – ECWA	Baghdad

Other United Nations Bodies

International Atomic Energy Agency – IAEA	Vienna
International Sea-Bed Authority	Kingston, Jamaica
Office of the United Nations Disaster Relief Co-Ordinator – UNDRO	Geneva
United Nations Centre for Human Settlements – HABITAT	Nairobi
United Nations Children's Fund – UNICEF	New York
United Nations Conference on Trade and Development – UNCTAD	Geneva
United Nations Development Programme – UNDP	New York
United Nations Environment Programme – UNEP	Nairobi
United Nations Fund for Population Activities – UNFPA	New York
United Nations High Commissioner for Refugees – UNHCR	Geneva
United Nations Industrial Development Organization – UNIDO	Vienna
United Nations Institute for Training and Research – UNITAR	New York
United Nations Observer Mission and Peace-keeping Forces in the Middle East	Jerusalem
United Nations Relief and Works Agency for Palestine Refugees in the Near East – UNRWA	Vienna
United Nations Research Institute for Social Development – UNRISD	Geneva
World Food Council – WFC	Rome
World Food Programme – WFP	Rome

Specialised Agencies within the UN System

Food and Agriculture Organization – FAO	Rome
General Agreement on Tariffs and Trade – GATT	Geneva
International Bank for Reconstruction and Development – IBRD (World Bank)	Washington, DC
International Development Association – IDA	Washington, DC
International Finance Corporation – IFC	Washington, DC
International Civil Aviation Organization – ICAO	Montreal
International Fund for Agricultural Development – IFAD	Rome
International Labour Organisation – ILO	Geneva
International Maritime Organization – IMO	London
International Monetary Fund – IMF	Washington, DC
International Telecommunication Union – ITU	Geneva

United Nations Education, Scientific and Cultural
  Organization – UNESCO   Paris
Universal Postal Union – UPU   Berne
World Health Organization – WHO   Geneva
World Intellectual Property Organization – WIPO   Geneva
World Meteorological Organization – WMO   Geneva

Warsaw Pact. Warsaw Treaty of Friendship, Co-operation and Mutual Assistance.

Members
Bulgaria   Czechoslovakia   East Germany   Hungary   Poland
Romania   Soviet Union

WCL. World Confederation of Labour. Links left-wing and communist trade unions. Based in Brussels.

Overwhelm means submerge utterly, crush, bring to sudden ruin. Majority votes, for example, seldom do any of these things.

P

People. Call them what they want to be called, short of festooning them with TITLES. Here are some common problems.

Yuri Andropov
Nnamdi Azikiwe
Malcolm Baldrige
Zbigniew Brzezinski
Leopoldo Calvo-Sotelo
Edward du Cann
Nicolae Ceausescu
Uncle Tom Cobbleigh
Poul Dalsager
Gaston Defferre
Lawrence Eagleburger
Prince Fahd
Garret FitzGerald
Gandhi
Hans-Dietrich Genscher
Felipe Gonzalez
Mikhail Gorbachev
Gurkha
Denis Healey
Junius Jayewardene
Lloyd's (insurance)
Lloyds (bank)
Pierre Mendès France
François Mitterrand
Daniel arap Moi

Muhammed (unless it is part of the name of someone who spells it differently)
Numeiri
Edgard Pisani
Qaddafi
Francis Pym
Andrei Sakharov
Sandinist (not Sandinista)
George Shultz,
  Charles Schultze
Soares (Portugal);
  Suarez (Spain)
Solzhenitsyn
Franz Josef Strauss
Tsar
Hans-Jochen Vogel
Caspar Weinberger

Dutch names
Van Agt
Den Uyl

German names
von

Some (not all) Indonesians have only one name (eg, Mr Suharto).

Percentages. Use the sign % instead of per cent. But write percentage, not %age. And write 5–6%, not 5%–6 or 5%–6%.

Places. Use English forms when they are in common use: Basle, Cologne, Leghorn, Lower Saxony, Lyons, Marseilles, Naples, Nuremberg, Turin. And English, always, rather than American: Rockefeller Centre, Pearl Harbour.
    Detailed lists of COUNTRIES and CITIES can be found elsewhere.
    Common problem names are these.

Argentina (adj and people
  Argentine, not Argentinian)
Baghdad

Bahrain
Bangladesh
Basle

BophuthaTswana
Cameroun
Cape Town
Caribbean
Colombia (South America)
Columbia (university, District
 of); British Columbia
Cracow
Dar es Salaam
Djibouti
Dominica (Caribbean island)
Dominican Republic (part of
 another island)
El Salvador, Salvadoran
Gettysburg
Gothenburg
Gurkha
Guyana (but French Guiana)
Harare
Hongkong
Jeddah
Kampuchea
KwaZulu

Luxembourg
Mauritania
Middlesbrough
North Rhine-Westphalia
Philippines (the people are
 Filipinos)
Phnom Penh
Pittsburgh
Reykjavik
Romania
St Antony's (college)
Salzburg
Sri Lanka
Strasbourg
Surinam
Taipei
Tehran
Teesside
The Gambia
Valetta
Württemberg
Yugoslavia

Plane. This is a tool or a surface. If it flies it is an aeroplane, aircraft or airliner.

Planets.

Name	Symbol	Distance from the sun in million miles
Sun	☉	0
Mercury	☿	36
Venus	♀	67
Earth	⊕	93
Mars	♂	142
Jupiter	♃	483
Saturn	♄	887
Uranus	♅	1,780
Neptune	♆	2,795
Pluto	♇	3,670

Plurals.

-oes

archipelagoes
cargoes
desperadoes
echoes
embargoes
haloes
heroes
innuendoes
manifestoes
mementoes
mosquitoes

mottoes
noes
potatoes
provisoes
salvoes
tomatoes
tornadoes
torpedoes
vetoes
volcanoes

-os

commandos
dynamos
embryos
folios
ghettos
impresarios
librettos
oratorios

peccadillos
pianos
radios
silos
solos
stilettos
studios

-eaus

bureaus
plateaus

-eaux

chateaux

-uses

buses
caucuses
circuses
focuses
geniuses
prospectuses

-i

termini
bacilli
nuclei
alumni
stimuli

-ums

conundrums
forums
nostrums
moratoriums
quorums
referendums
stadiums
ultimatums
vacuums

-a

consortia
corrigenda
crematoria
data
media
memoranda
phenomena
quanta
sanatoria
strata

-ves	**-fs**
hooves	dwarfs
scarves	roofs
wharves	turfs

-as	**-ae**
agendas	formulae

Note: **indexes** (of books), but **indices** (indicators, index numbers).

Presently means **soon**, not **at present**. Thus: **Presently Kep opened the door of the shed, and let out Jemima Puddle-Duck.**

Prevaricate means evade the truth; **procrastinate** means put off.

Problem. The problem with problem is it is overused, so much so that it is becoming a problem word.

Proofreader's marks. These are the main proofreader's marks recommended by the British Standards Institution. Most printers and editors have their own slight variations.

Proofreader's marks

General

Instruction	Textual mark	Marginal mark	Notes
Correction is concluded	None	/	Make after each correction
Leave unchanged	−−−−−− under characters to remain	(√)	
Remove extraneous marks	Encircle marks to be removed	✕	e.g. film or paper edges visible between lines on bromide or diazo proofs
Push down risen spacing material	Encircle blemish	⊥	
Refer to appropriate authority anything of doubtful accuracy	Encircle word(s) affected	(?)	

Deletion, insertion and substitution

Instruction	Textual mark	Marginal mark	Notes
Insert in text the matter indicated in the margin	ʎ	New matter followed by ʎ	
Insert additional matter identified by a letter in a diamond	ʎ	ʎ Followed by for example ◇A	The relevant section of the copy should be supplied with the corresponding letter marked on it in a diamond e.g. ◇A
Delete	/ through character(s) or ⊢—⊣ through words to be deleted	♂	
Delete and close up	͡/ through character or through characters e.g. charaäcter charaäcter	♂	

68

Instruction	Textual mark	Marginal mark	Notes
Substitute character or substitute part of one or more word(s)	/ through character or ⊢————⊣ through word(s)	New character or new word(s)	
Wrong fount. Replace by character(s) of correct fount	Encircle character(s) to be changed	⊗	
Change damaged character(s)	Encircle character(s) to be changed	✕	
Set in or change to italic	———— under character(s) to be set or changed	⊔⊔	Where space does not permit textual marks encircle the affected area instead
Set in or change to capital letters	≡≡≡ under character(s) to be set or changed	≡	
Set in or change to small capital letters	≡≡ under character(s) to be set or changed	=	
Set in or change to capital letters for initial letters and small capital letters for the rest of the words	≡ under initial letters and ≡≡ under rest of the word(s)	≣	
Set in or change to bold type	∿∿∿ under character(s) to be set or changed	∿	
Set in or change to bold italic type	∿∿∿ under character(s) to be set or'changed	⊔⊔∿	
Change capital letters to lower case letters	Encircle character(s) to be changed	≢	

Instruction	Textual mark	Marginal mark	Notes
Change small capital letters to lower case letters	Encircle character(s) to be changed	≠	
Change italic to upright type	Encircle character(s) to be changed	⊔	
Invert type	Encircle character to be inverted	↻	
Substitute or insert character in 'superior' position	/ through character or ⅄ where required	⌐ under character e.g. ²	
Substitute or insert character in 'inferior' position	/ through character or ⅄ where required	L over character e.g. ²	
Substitute ligature e.g. ffi for separate letters	⊢———⊣ through characters affected	⌣ e.g. ffi	
Substitute separate letters for ligature	⊢———⊣	Write out separate letters	
Substitute or insert full stop or decimal point	/ through character or ⅄ where required	⊙	
Substitute or insert colon	/ through character or ⅄ where required	⊙	
Substitute or insert semi-colon	/ through character or ⅄ where required	;	

Instruction	Textual mark	Marginal mark	Notes
Substitute or insert oblique	/ through character or ⅄ where required		

Positioning and spacing

Instruction	Textual mark	Marginal mark	Notes
Start new paragraph			
Run on (no new paragraph)			
Transpose characters or words	between characters or words, numbered when necessary		
Transpose a number of characters or words	3 2 1	1 2 3	The vertical strokes are made through the characters or words to be transposed and numbered in the correct sequence
Transpose lines			
Transpose a number of lines	——— 3 ——— 2 ——— 1		Rules extend from the margin into the text with each line to be transplanted numbered in the correct sequence
Centre	enclosing matter to be centred	[ ]	
Indent			Give the amount of the indent in the marginal mark

R

Reason. **Because** usually has no place in sentences involving the word **reason**. The reason is **that** it is redundant. **That** is the word. **That** should also be used after **reason** on many occasions when the temptation is to use **why**. The reason you think you should always write **the reason why** is your familiarity with the title "The Reason Why". But that book takes its name from Tennyson's "Their's not to reason why", where **reason** is being used as a verb.

Regions. See STATES.

Richter scale. See EARTHQUAKES.

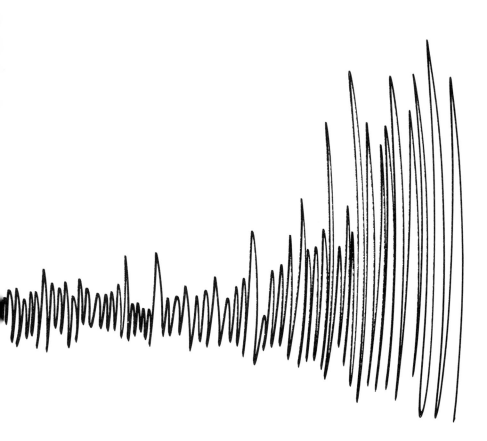

S

Scotch. To scotch means to **disable**, not to **destroy** (**We have scotched the snake, not killed it**). The people are also **Scotch**, except for some among them who call themselves **Scots** or **Scottish**; choose as you like.

Semi-colons. Semi-colons should be used to mark a pause longer than a comma and shorter than a full stop.

Use them to distinguish phrases listed after a colon if commas will not do the job clearly. Thus, **They agreed on only three points: the ceasefire should be immediate; it should be internationally supervised, preferably by the** OAU; **and a peace conference should be held, either in Geneva or in Ouagadougou.**

Short words. Use them. They are often Anglo-Saxon rather than Latin in origin. They are easy to spell and easy to understand. Thus prefer **about** to **approximately, after** to **following, let** to **permit, but** to **however, use** to **utilise, make** to **manufacture, plant** to **facility, take part** to **participate, set up** to **establish, enough** to **sufficient, show** to **demonstrate** and so on. **Underdeveloped** countries are often better described as **poor; substantive** usually means **real** or **big**.

Simplistic. Prefer **simple-minded, naive.**

Slang. Slang, like metaphors, should be used only occasionally if it is to have effect. Avoid expressions used only by journalists, such as giving people the **thumbs up**, the **thumbs down** or the **green light**. Stay clear of **gravy trains** and **salami tactics**. Do not use **the likes of**. And avoid words and expressions that are ugly or overused, such as the **bottom line, caring** (as an adjective), **guesstimate** (use **guess**), **schizophrenic** (unless the context is medical), **option** (prefer **choice**), **crisis, key, major, massive, meaningful, muscular, perceptions, prestigious, problem** and **overwhelm**.

Spelling. English rather than anything else (thus, Sandinist not Sandinista). Never American (so Labour not Labor, except the Australian Labor party, which is spelt that way even though Australians spell labour as we do).

Use -ise, -isation (realise, organisation) throughout. We do not hospitalise, however.

Follow the preferred practice of companies or individuals themselves in writing their names.

For spelling rules for place names, see PLACES (with detailed specific lists under COUNTRIES; CITIES; and STATES, REGIONS, PROVINCES, COUNTIES).

For spelling rules for other proper names, see PEOPLE and COM-PANIES. Other common difficulties are listed below (and see also -ABLE, -EABLE, -IBLE).

Spell these words the way they are shown here.

accommodate
acknowledgment
adviser, advisory
aeroplane, aircraft, airliner,
   not plane
aesthetic
Afrikaans (the language),
   Afrikaner (the person)
aging (like caging, paging,
   raging, waging)
balk (not baulk)
bandwagon
battalion
benefited
biased
block (never bloc)
bogey (bogie is on a
   locomotive)
burnt
bused, busing
by-election, by-law,
   by-product
bye (in sport only)
channelled
checking account (spell it
   thus when explaining to
   Americans a current
   account, which is to be
   preferred)
commemorate
connection
consensus
defendant
dependant (person),
   dependent (adj)
desiccation
detente (not détente)
Deutschemark
dexterous (not dextrous)
disk (in a computer context),
   otherwise disc

dispatch (not despatch)
dispel, dispelling
distil, distiller
divergences
dwelt
dyeing (colour)
dyke
embarrass (but harass)
encyclopedia
enroll, enrolment
ensure (make certain), insure
   (against risks)
farther (distance), further
   (additional)
Filipino (person), Philippine
   (adj of the Philippines)
flier, high-flier
focused, focusing
foetus
forbear (abstain), forebear
   (ancestor)
forbid
foreboding
foreclose
forefather
forestall
forewarn
forgather
forgo (do without), forego
   (precede)
forsake
forsworn
fulfil, fulfilling
fullness
fulsome
grey
guerrilla
gypsy
harass (but embarrass)
hiccough
high-tech

incur, incurring
innocuous
inoculate
inquire, inquiry (not
   enquire, enquiry)
hallo (not hello)
hodge-podge
hurrah, not hooray
install, instalment,
   installation
instil, instilling
intransigent
jail (not gaol)
jewellery (not jewelry)
judgment
labelled
laisser-faire
learnt
levelled
libelled
licence (noun), license
   (verb)
linchpin, lynch law
literal, littoral (shore)
loth (reluctant), loathe (hate),
   loathsome
manoeuvre(-vring)
medieval
mileage
millennium
minuscule
Muslim (not Moslem)
naivety
nonplussed
occur, occurring
paediatric(ian)
pastime
pedlar (not peddler)
phoney (not phony)
piggy-back
pigmy
politburo
practice (noun), practise
   (verb)

principal (head; loan; or
   adjective), principle
   (abstract noun)
processer
program (only in a computer
   context), otherwise
   programme
recur, recurrent, recurring
sacrilegious
sanatorium
seize
siege
skulduggery
smelt
smidgen (not smidgeon)
smooth (both noun and verb)
soothe
soyabean
specialty (only in context of
   medicine, steel and
   chemicals), otherwise
   speciality
spelt
spoilt
storey (floor)
stratagem
strategy
superseded
swap (not swop)
synonym
telephone (not phone)
television (not TV)
threshold
trade union, trade unions
   (but Trades Union
   Congress)
transAtlantic
travelled
vaccinate
vacillate
withhold
word processer
wry, wrily

Standard International Trade Classification. See COMMODITIES AND MANUFACTURED GOODS.

States, regions, provinces, counties. Here are the correct spellings of the main administrative subdivisions of industrialised countries.

America (United States of America): States

Alabama	Montana
Alaska	Nebraska
Arizona	Nevada
Arkansas	New Hampshire
California	New Jersey
Colorado	New Mexico
Connecticut	New York
Delaware	North Carolina
Florida	North Dakota
Georgia	Ohio
Hawaii	Oklahoma
Idaho	Oregon
Illinois	Pennsylvania
Indiana	Rhode Island
Iowa	South Carolina
Kansas	South Dakota
Kentucky	Tennessee
Louisiana	Texas
Maine	Utah
Maryland	Vermont
Massachusetts	Virginia
Michigan	Washington
Minnesota	West Virginia
Mississippi	Wisconsin
Missouri	Wyoming

Australia (Commonwealth of Australia)
States: New South Wales   Queensland   South Australia   Western Australia   Tasmania   Victoria

Territories: Northern Territory   Australian Capital Territory

Belgium (Kingdom of Belgium): Provinces
Antwerp   Brabant   East Flanders   Hainaut   Liège   Limburg   Luxembourg   Namur   West Flanders

Brazil (United States of Brazil): States

Acre	Pernambuco
Alagoas	Piauí
Amazonas	Rio de Janeiro
Bahia	Rio Grande do Norte
Ceará	Rio Grande do Sul
Espírito Santo	Rondônia
Goiás	Santa Catarina
Maranhão	São Paulo
Mato Grosso	Sergipe
Mato Grosso do Sul	Federal Territories
Minas Gerais	Amapá
Pará	Roraima
Paraíba	Federal District (Distrito Federal)
Paraná	

Note: These spellings are included for reference. As a general rule, do not use accents on Portuguese words.

Canada

Provinces	Territories
Alberta	Northwest Territories
British Columbia	Yukon Territory
Manitoba	
New Brunswick	
Newfoundland	
Nova Scotia	
Ontario	
Prince Edward Island	
Quebec	
Saskatchewan	

France: Regions

Alsace	Ile-de-France
Aquitaine	Languedoc-Roussillon
Auvergne	Limousin
Basse-Normandie	Lorraine
Brittany (Bretagne)	Midi-Pyrénées
Burgundy (Bourgogne)	Nord-Pas-de-Calais
Centre	Pays de la Loire
Champagne-Ardennes	Picardy (Picardie)
Corsica (Corse)	Poitou-Charentes
Franche-Comté	Provence-Alpes-Côte d'Azur
Haute-Normandie	Rhône-Alpes

West Germany (Federal Republic of Germany): States

(in German, Länder)
Baden-Württemberg
Bavaria (Bayern)
Bremen
Hamburg
Hesse (Hessen)
Lower Saxony (Niedersachsen)

North Rhine-Westphalia
  (Nordrhein-Westfalen)
Rhineland-Palatinate
  (Rheinland-Pfalz)
Saarland
Schleswig-Holstein
West Berlin

Holland (Kingdom of the Netherlands): Provinces

Drenthe
Dronten
Friesland
Gelderland
Groningen
Lelystad
Limburg

Noord-Brabant
Noord-Holland
Overijssel
Utrecht
Zeeland
Zuid-Holland
Zuideijke Ijsselmeerpolders

Ireland

Provinces	*Counties*
Connacht	Galway
	Leitrim
	Mayo
	Roscommon
	Sligo
Leinster	Carlow
	Dublin
	Kildare
	Kilkenny
	Laoighis
	Longford
	Louth
	Meath
	Offaly
	Westmeath
	Wexford
	Wicklow
Munster	Clare
	Cork
	Kerry
	Limerick
	Tipperary, North Riding, South Riding
	Waterford
Ulster	Cavan
	Donegal
	Monaghan

Italy (Republic of Italy): Regions

Abruzzi
Basilicata
Calabria
Campania
Emilia-Romagna
Friuli-Venezia Giulia
Lazio
Liguria
Lombardy (Lombardia)
Marche

Molise
Piedmont (Piemonte)
Puglia
Sardinia (Sardegna)
Sicily (Sicilia)
Tuscany (Toscana)
Trentino-Alto Adige
Umbria
Valle d'Aosta
Veneto

Soviet Union (Union of Soviet Socialist Republics): Union Republics

Armenian Soviet Socialist
  Republic (SSR)
Azerbaidzhan SSR
Byelorussian SSR
Estonian SSR
Georgian SSR
Kazakh SSR
Kirghiz SSR

Latvian SSR
Lithuanian SSR
Moldavian SSR
Russian SFSR
Tadzhik SSR
Turkmen SSR
Ukrainian SSR
Uzbek SSR

Autonomous Republics
Within RSFSR:
  Bashkir
  Buryat
  Chechen-Ingush
  Chuvash
  Daghestan
  Kabardino-Balkar
  Kalmyk
  Karelian
Within Azerbaidzhan:
  Nakhichevan
Within Georgia:
  Abkhasian
Within Uzbekistan:
  Kara-Kalpak

Komi
Mari
Mordovian
North Ossetian
Tatar
Tuva
Udmurt
Yakut

Adzhar

Autonomous Regions
Within RSFSR:
  Adygei
  Gorno-Altai
  Jewish

Kharachayevo-Cherkess
Khakass

Within Azerbaidzhan:
Nagorno-Karabakh
Within Georgia:
South Ossetian

Within Tadzhikistan:
Gorno-Badakhshan

United Kingdom
England: Non-Metropolitan Counties

Avon
Bedfordshire
Berkshire
Buckinghamshire
Cambridgeshire
Cheshire
Cleveland
Cornwall/Isles of Scilly
Cumbria
Derbyshire
Devon
Dorset
Durham
East Sussex
Essex
Gloucestershire
Hampshire
Hereford & Worcestershire
Hertfordshire
Humberside

Isle of Wight
Kent
Lancashire
Leicestershire
Lincolnshire
Norfolk
Northamptonshire
Northumberland
North Yorkshire
Nottinghamshire
Oxfordshire
Shropshire
Somerset
Staffordshire
Suffolk
Surrey
Tyne & Wear
Warwickshire
West Sussex
Wiltshire

Wales
Clwyd
Dyfed
Gwent
Gwynedd

Mid Glamorgan
Powys
South Glamorgan
West Glamorgan

Scotland: Regions
Highland
Grampian
Tayside
Fife
Lothian
Borders
Central
Strathclyde
Dumfries and Galloway

Islands Area:
Orkney
Shetland
Western Isles

Northern Ireland: Districts

Ards	Magherafelt
Belfast	Moyle
Castlereagh	Newtownabbey
Down	Armagh
Lisburn	Banbridge
North Down	Craigavon
Antrim	Dungannon
Ballymena	Newry and Mourne
Ballymoney	Fermanagh
Carrickfergus	Limavady
Coleraine	Londonderry
Cookstown	Omagh
Larne	Strabane

Stock Market Indices
The Financial Times Ordinary Share Index (the 30 Share Index) consists of the following.

Allied-Lyons
ASDA-MFI Group
Beecham Group
BICC
Blue Circle Industries
BOC Group
Boots Co.
British Petroleum Co.
British Telecommunications
BTR
Cadbury Schweppes
Courtaulds
General Electric
Glaxo Holdings
Grand Metropolitan
Guest, Keen & Nettlefolds

Guinness
Hanson Trust
Hawker Siddeley Group
Imperial Chemical Industries
Lucas Industries
Marks & Spencer
National Westminster Bank
Peninsular & Oriental
 Steam Navigation Co.
Plessey Co.
Royal Insurance
Tate & Lyle
Thorn EMI
Trusthouse Forte
Vickers

The Financial Times Stock Exchange 100 Share Index consists of the following.

Abbey Life Group
Allied-Lyons
Argyll Group
ASDA-MFI Group
Associated British Foods
Bank of Scotland
 (Governor and Co. of)
Barclays Bank
Bass
B.A.T Industries
Beecham Group
BET
BICC
Blue Circle Industries
BOC Group
Boots Co.
BPB Industries
British & Commonwealth
 Shipping Co.
British Aerospace
British Petroleum Co.
British Telecommunications
Britoil

BTR
Burton Group
Cable & Wireless
Cadbury Schweppes
Coates Viyella
Commercial Union Assurance
Consolidated Gold Fields
Cookson Group
Courtaulds
Dee Corp.
Distillers Co.
Dixons Group
English China Clays
Ferranti
Fisons
General Accident Fire &
 Life Assurance Corp.
General Electric Co.
Glaxo Holdings
Globe Investment Trust
Granada Group
Grand Metropolitan
Great Universal Stores

Guardian Royal Exchange
Guest, Keen & Nettlefolds
Guinness
Hammerson Property
 Investment & Development
 Corp.
Hanson Trust
Hawker Siddeley Group
Imperial Chemical Industries
Jaguar
Ladbroke Group
Land Securities
Legal & General Group
Lloyds Bank
Lonrho
Lucas Industries
Marks & Spencer
MEPC
Midland Bank
National Westminster Bank
Northern Foods
Peninsular & Oriental Steam
 Navigation Co.
Pearson
Pilkington Brothers
Plessey Co.
Prudential Corp.
Racal Electronics
Ranks Hovis McDougall
Rank Organisation
Reckitt & Colman
Redland

Reed International
Reuters Holdings
Rio Tinto-Zinc Corp.
RMC Group
Rowntree Mackintosh
Royal Bank of Scotland Group
Royal Insurance
J. Sainsbury
Scottish & Newcastle
 Breweries
Sears
Sedgwick Group
Shell Transport & Trading
Smith & Nephew Associated
 Companies
Smiths Industries
Standard Chartered Bank
Standard Telephones & Cables
Storehouse
Sun Alliance and London
 Insurance
Tarmac
Tesco
Thorn EMI
Trafalgar House
Trusthouse Forte
Unilever
United Biscuits (Holdings)
Wellcome
Whitbread & Co.
Willis Faber
Woolworth Holdings

The Dow-Jones Industrial Average consists of the following.
Allied-Signal
Aluminum Co. of America (ALCOA)
American Can Company
American Express Co.
American Telephone & Telegraph Co.
Bethlehem Steel Corp.
Chevron Corp.
E. I. du Pont de Nemours & Co.
Eastman Kodak Co.
Exxon Corp.
General Electric Co.

The Dow-Jones Industrial Average—continued
General Motors Corp.
The Goodyear Tire & Rubber Company
Inco Limited
International Business Machines Corp.
International Harvester Co.
International Paper Co.
McDonald's Corp.
Merck & Co.
Minnesota Mining & Mfg. Co.
Owens-Illinois
Philip Morris Companies
Procter & Gamble Co.
Sears, Roebuck and Co.
Texaco
Union Carbide Corp.
United Technologies Corp.
United States Steel Corp.
Westinghouse Electric Corp.
F. W. Woolworth Co.

T

Titles. In bodymatter, the names of all living people should be preceded by Mr, Mrs, Miss or some other title, except occasionally on first mention when plain Ronald Reagan, Margaret Thatcher or other appropriate combination of first name and surname will do. Titles are not necessary in headings or captions, or for dead people (except, perhaps, **Dr Johnson** and **Mr Gladstone**), but in general do not refer to people in headings and captions by their first names only.

Take care with foreign titles. Malaysian ones are so confusing that it is wise to dispense with them altogether. Do not, however, call **Tunku Abdul Rahman Mr Abdul Rahman**; refer to him, on each mention, as **Abdul Rahman**. Avoid, above all, **Mr Tunku Abdul Rahman**.

Use **Dr** for qualified medical people, and occasionally in book reviews and the science section when the correct alternative is not known.

If you use a title, get it right. **Rear-Admiral** Jones should not be called **Admiral** Jones.

Professor X, President Y, and the **Rev John Z** may be **Mr, Mrs** or **Miss** on second mention.

On first mention use forename and surname; thereafter drop forename (unless there are two people with the same surname mentioned in the article).
Mr Norman Tebbit then **Mr Tebbit**.

Avoid nicknames unless the person is always known (or prefers to be known) by one:
Mr Tony Benn   Mr Tiny Rowland   Mr Tip O'Neill.

Avoid the American habit of joining office and name:
Prime Minister Thatcher   Chancellor Kohl.

Avoid middle initials. Nobody will confuse **John F. Kennedy** with **John P. Kennedy** or **John R. Kennedy.**

And avoid **Ms** if possible. Married women who are known by their maiden names – eg, Jane Fonda – are **Miss**, unless they have made it clear that they want to be called something else.

Rules for capital letters in titles can be found under capitals.

U

Unlike should not be followed by **in**.

Unnecessary words. Some words add nothing but length to your prose. Use adjectives to make your meaning more precise and be cautious of those you find yourself using to make it more emphatic. The word **very** is a case in point. If it occurs in a sentence you have written, try leaving it out and see whether the meaning is changed. **He was tall** may have more force than **He was very tall.**

Avoid **strike action** (**strike** will do), the **business community** (**businessmen**), **cutbacks** (**cuts**), **track record** (**record**), **wilderness areas** (**wild areas**), **large-scale** (**big**), **shower activity** (**rain**), **weather conditions** (**weather**), etc.

Use words with care: a **heart condition** is usually a **bad heart, positive thoughts** (held by long-suffering creditors, according to *The Economist*) presumably means **optimism**, a **substantially finished** bridge is an **unfinished** bridge, a **major speech** usually just a **speech**. Something with **reliability problems** probably **does not work**.

Upper case. See CAPITALS.

V

Verbal. Every agreement, except the nod-and-wink variety, is **verbal**. If you mean that one was not written down, describe it as **oral**.

W

Warn is transitive, so you must either **give warning** or **warn somebody**.

Weights and measures. See MEASURES.

Which informs, **that** defines. **This is the house that Jack built.** But **This house, which Jack built, is now falling down. Which** can, however, be used to relieve a sentence already loaded with **thats**, eg, **He recalled that that was the day that he had returned to the family which he had abandoned.**

Wind speed. The Beaufort Scale (see page 89), once a picturesque fleet of well-scrubbed men o'war and fishing smacks, has been rendered bland by the World Meteorological Organisation.

Force	Description	Conditions (abbreviated) on land	Conditions (abbreviated) at sea	Equivalent speed at 10 metres height knots	miles per hour	metres per second
0	Calm	Smoke rises vertically	Sea like a mirror	less than 1	less than 1	0.0–0.2
1	Light air	Smoke drifts	Ripples	1–3	1–3	0.3–1.5
2	Light breeze	Leaves rustle	Small wavelets	4–6	4–7	1.7–3.3
3	Gentle breeze	Wind extends light flag	Large wavelets, crests break	7–10	8–12	3.4–5.4
4	Moderate breeze	Raises paper and dust	Small waves, some white horses	11–16	13–18	5.5–7.9
5	Fresh breeze	Small trees in leaf sway	Moderate waves, many white horses	17–21	19–24	8.0–10.7
6	Strong breeze	Large branches in motion	Large waves form, some spray	22–27	25–31	10.8–13.8
7	Near gale	Whole trees in motion	Sea heaps up, white foam streaks	28–33	32–38	13.9–17.1
8	Gale	Breaks twigs off trees	Moderately high waves, well-marked foam streaks	34–40	39–46	17.2–20.7
9	Strong gale	Slight structural damage	High waves, crests start to tumble over	41–47	47–54	20.8–24.4
10	Storm	Trees uprooted, considerable structural damage	Very high waves, white sea tumbles	48–55	55–63	24.5–28.4
11	Violent storm	Very rarely experienced, widespread damage	Exceptionally high waves, edges of wave crests blown to froth	56–63	64–72	28.5–32.6
12	Hurricane	—	Sea completely white with driving spray	64 & over	73 & over	32.7–over

Y

Yachting. Initial letters preceding the sail numbers in international classes are allocated in this way.

A – Argentina
B – Belgium
BL – Brazil
BU – Bulgaria
CY – Ceylon
CZ – Czechoslovakia
D – Denmark
E – Spain
F – France
G – West Germany
GE – Greece
GO – East Germany
H – Holland
I – Italy
J – Japan
K – Britain
KA – Australia
KB – Bermuda
KC – Canada
KK – Kenya
KS – Singapore
KZ – New Zealand

L – Finland
M – Hungary
MD – Monaco
N – Norway
OE – Austria
P – Portugal
PH – Philippines
PZ – Poland
RC – Cuba
RI – Indonesia
RM – Romania
S – Sweden
SA – South Africa
SR – Soviet Union
TK – Turkey
U – Uruguay
US – America
V – Venezuela
X – Chile
Y – Yugoslavia
Z – Switzerland

Sources and additional reading

The reference material in this Style Book is largely drawn from books bearing *The Economist* imprint.

Crawford's Directory of City Connections lists quoted, USM, OTC and large private companies and their management; also lists their advisers such as stockbrokers, merchant banks, solicitors and auditors. Lists the clients of over 4,000 firms of professional advisers.

Economic Statistics 1900–1983 brings together a historical series of economic indicators for six main industrial countries (Britain, America, France, Germany, Italy, Japan). Tables of national output and expenditure, personal income and profits, trade, balance of payments, finance, prices and population.

Pocket Accountant is an A–Z of accounting phrases, defining terms ranging from auditing to inventory, extraordinary items to goodwill. Explains the role of the professional bodies and accounting regulators on both sides of the Atlantic.

Pocket Banker, a dictionary of international banking, finance and international institutions.

The Pocket Economist is another A–Z of economic terms, explained with words, charts, tables and cartoons. In 194 pages, it is a guided tour of economics, economic institutions and high finance in Britain and America.

Pocket Guide to Defence is a dictionary of important defence issues: national interest, big business, politics. Explains terms such as VX, Trip-Wire, threshold.

Pocket Guide to Marketing is an A–Z format pocket book that summarises marketing jargon and techniques.

Pocket International Directory and Address Book contains the following information for 26 countries: addresses, telex and telephone numbers for government, international and national organisations, both central and regional; business, finance, trade and labour organisations; travel, accommodation, the media; clubs and theatres; and inter-country dialling codes.

World Business Cycles compiles and analyses fluctuations in gross domestic product, share prices, money stocks and interest rates.

The World in Figures covers over 200 countries. Provides comparative worldwide figures on everything from population and commodity production to finance and external trade. Also analyses individual countries, with sub-sections on people, resources, equipment, production, finance and external trade.

The World Measurement Guide defines, converts and illustrates national and international measures and statistics, system by system and industry by industry. Includes: conversions, space and time, agriculture, forestry and fishing, practical definitions and formulae (for statistics, economics, insurance, investment, etc), currencies, fractions to decimals, percentage reversals, reciprocals, percentages, multiplications and interest rates.

Additional reading

Oxford Dictionary for Writers and Editors, compiled by the Oxford English Dictionary Department. 1st ed. 1981

The Complete Plain Words by Sir Ernest Gowers, Penguin Books

Dictionary of Modern English Usage by H. W. Fowler. 2nd Edition revised by Sir Ernest Gowers, Oxford University Press

The Europa Year Book (2 volumes), Europa Publications Ltd

Hart's Rules for Compositors and Readers at the University Press, Oxford, Oxford University Press

Jane's All the World's Aircraft, Jane's Publishing Co.

Jane's Fighting Ships, Jane's Publishing Co.

Index

Notes